how
to form
your own
PROFESSIONAL
CORPORATION

by
Ted
Nicholas

First Printing — September, 1977

Library of Congress Number — 77-00060
International Standard Book Number — 0-913864-13-7

Published by:
ENTERPRISE PUBLISHING CO.
Suite 501
Beneficial Building
Market Street
Wilmington, Delaware 19801

To my beloved Luanne

Acknowledgments

The author wishes to thank the Secretaries of State, of all the States in the Union and their Corporation Departments, for their cooperation and contributions in the preparation of the materials and data included in this book; and for their helpful suggestions in the development of the Universal forms contained in this book.

Table of Contents

Foreword

Imagine that! You are at the point of considering an important business decision, and you find the CPA-consultant with 22 years experience in the practice of public accounting is commencing the foreword to the book *HOW TO FORM YOUR OWN PROFESSIONAL CORPORATION* with a discussion of philosophy.

Yes, indeed I am. Consider the following case which, though a fictionalized example, is unfortunately representative of many examples taking place every day in this country. The example refers to a physician but applies equally to all professionals.

In the morning, Dr. Brown enters the operating room of Town Hospital and performs delicate brain surgery on the young daughter of the Mayor. The operation is a success. Interns and nurses stand in awe of Dr. Brown's brilliance,

skill, and his steady hand in the face of an operation which turned out to be more delicate than had been anticipated.

Early in the afternoon, Dr. Brown gives a seminar to the staff of Town Hospital on the care of patients. He explains that the staff must be both efficient and compassionate. He reminds them that they are dealing with human beings who, in addition to having temperatures and blood pressure readings, also have thoughts and feelings. He stresses that the staff must talk *and listen to* the patients. He points out that paying attention to what the patient says does more than help the morale of the patient; it may also help in learning more about the patient's malady. Says Dr. Brown: "The patient is telling you something. Remember, the patient alone knows when it hurts, where it hurts, and how intensely it hurts. The patient alone

i

knows how he will feel about certain things. All of this knowledge can help the patient in two ways — it can improve his psychological frame of mind, and it can lead to improved medical treatment."

At the conclusion of the seminar, the staff marvels at Dr. Brown's professional knowledge, his awareness of human psychology, and his super ability to communicate tremendous knowledge to the Town Hospital staff, while continuing to treat them as equals.

At 4:30 p.m., Dr. Brown shows up at a meeting with his attorney and CPA to consider whether to incorporate his medical practice. After listening inattentively for half an hour, Dr. Brown states: "This is all over my head. You people are the professionals in this matter. I have neither the patience nor the knowledge to participate in this decision. You people decide, draw up the necessary papers, and tell me where to sign. Now, if you'll excuse me . . ." And Dr. Brown leaves the room. And he leaves the plans for his financial future in the hands of others.

The attorney and CPA will do their best to decide what they believe to be best for Dr. Brown. However, it is Dr. Brown who must live with the consequences of their decision. It is his hard-earned money which might be needlessly paid to the insatiable tax-collector. It is he who will be left with the discomfort or satisfaction of whatever the decisions are. And we are not merely talking of just one decision — whether or not to incorporate; there are many, many decisions to be made. And on all of these matters, by default, Dr. Brown has chosen not to participate in the planning of his future.

It has been my experience that many financial professional advisors much prefer discussing matters with an informed, interested client. It has several advantages. We can find out what your goals are; we can discuss *in advance* how you might react to many of the good and bad points which can be anticipated along the way; we can, by discussion, reduce the number of surprises which you will encounter along the way; and, of course, you can tell us "where it hurts."

You may happen to run into a professional who admonishes you: "This is a very complex matter, Doctor. I suggest that you go back to your dentistry, and leave these financial/legal/insurance (or whatever) decisions to me." I would suggest that you change advisors immediately. It's your life, your money, and your future which will be affected beneficially or adversely as a result of the decisions. Pay attention, become informed, and participate!

And now let's discuss *HOW TO FORM YOUR OWN PROFESSIONAL CORPORATION.* The book you hold in your hands is significantly different from most of the books and articles I have seen on Professional Corporations. Most of them come on hard with a built-in conclusion as to the decision which you should eventually make. If the pitch is to incorporate, there will be a few token paragraphs of the disadvantages.

HOW TO FORM YOUR OWN PROFESSIONAL CORPORATION clearly acknowledges that there is no categorical answer which suits all professionals. Mr. Nicholas recognizes that the decisions made in this area are extremely important for you to study and evaluate. If you choose to confer with professionals after reading this book, you will be better-informed for the discussion, you can knowledgeably participate in the decision, and will undoubtedly save the fees you would pay to your advisor to explain to you the basics. Furthermore, because Mr. Nicholas has explored many aspects of this question, and his given an in-depth analysis of both advantages and disadvantages, you can approach your decisions with a balance of opinion. Your professional advisor, as a result of his own biased opinion and without any intent to deny you full knowledge, may present to you only one side of the questions. The advanced study and preparation by you will allow you to consider more aspects of the important topics at hand, to make additional observations, and to ask pertinent questions. It will be a benefit to both you and your professional advisor. As Mr. Nicholas aptly points out (page 11) ". . . the more you learn before approaching professional help, the less you will have to pay for it."

Almost as a fringe bonus, if you decide to proceed with incorporation, all necessary forms are included in this book.

For most of the readers, I have never met you, and am unfamiliar with your life goals and financial situations. Consequently, I cannot possibly express an opinion about whether or not you should incorporate. However, I can without reservation most strongly recomment that you inform yourself about the subject. Read and study *HOW TO FORM YOUR OWN PROFESSIONAL CORPORATION*. Evaluate what you have read. Then you will be in a knowledgeable position to decide on your next step. Good luck!

Sincerely,

Robert A. Steiner, CPA

Definition of a Professional Corporation

A professional corporation is a licensed professional practice organized for business purposes into the corporate form.

Professional corporations may provide any professional service for which a license or other authority issued by a state is prerequisite to rendering the service in that state. With few exceptions, a professional corporation is limited by law to the practice of one profession only.

Some of the professions that fall within the scope of professional corporation law are included in alphabetical order:

— Accountancy
— Architecture
— Certified Shorthand Reporters
— Certified Social Workers
— Dentistry
— Dental Hygienists
— Engineering
— Funeral Directors
— Landscape Architecture
— Land Surveying
— Law
— Life Insurance Agent
— Medicine and Surgery
— Pharmacy
— Physical Therapy
— Psychology
— Veterinary Medicine

Introduction

You are a licensed professional — in private practice -- a respected, responsible, reasonably successful member of your community. They say, in fact, that you're on top of the heap, socially and financially. Socially, you might not argue with this statement; it's not all that important to you anyway. But financially? You might wonder about those tables that place you in the top 10 percent of incomes. If you're so successful, why aren't you more satisfied? You know the answer, of course.

If you could spend your so-called discretionary income at the same level as Mr. Average, you would be fairly well off. If you paid the same percentage of your income in taxes as he, you would be *very* well off. And, if in addition, you could enjoy the security of a retirement plan that was proportionately as good as his, you would really be King of the Mountain. You could feel truly satisfied that the big investment you made to get you where you are was being repaid.

That, however, is not the way it is. You are subject to pressures that are almost unknown to the fellow grossing fourteen thousand — pressures to give more to innumerable worthy causes, to maintain certain standards set for you by your peers and society at large, to give your children at least a start toward the same standards. If you had to pay only 20 percent of your taxable income to the government instead of twice that much or even more, you would have ample reason to be satisfied. And if you could feel that a part of your before-tax income was being built up in a retirement fund in the same ratio to your income as that of persons in the 20 percent bracket, you could accept much more easily your classification as the affluent ten percent.

You are aware (vaguely or acutely) that there are legal ways to retain more of your income than you now keep. You know that one way is through incorporation, but that just frustrates you, since you are a professional, not a business person. At the university, they didn't teach you about the business aspects of your profession. Even if they had attempted to teach you this, there was enough learning to absorb merely studying the professional side of your future practice. You have probably realized, however, that there is no escaping the study of business for anyone seriously interested in safeguarding his treasure. You may hire business experts to do it for you, but you will still need a good understanding of business yourself.

Many professionals who have overcome their unfamiliarity with business have found that through incorporating their practice, they can enjoy the same kind of tax treatment as incorporated businesspeople. This book takes you right to the heart of the incorporation question, gives you the important considerations in favor of and against incorporating, so that you can reach a decision quickly and more intelligently.

The probability is that you can increase your net income by incorporating. That certainly has been the trend in business, and now it has also become the trend in the professions. Improvement of their financial position is the obvious reason for incorporation for both businesspeople and professionals. It is no guarantee, however. Corporations fail as well as other forms of business. A professional corporation, on the other hand, is less likely than a business corporation to get into trouble from underfinancing or low sales volume. If the professional corporation does run into trouble, it will more likely be through inattention to the business side of the practice and a resulting session with the Internal Revenue Service. That might sound as though success for the professional corporation is merely a matter of hiring a good attorney and an equally good accountant to pay attention to the business details, while the corporation members go their professional way. Hiring good people to help keep you out of trouble is often a fine idea. But you'll need more than that.

You and your fellow directors of the corporation, if any, will have much more to do than distribute the income once a year and pick out the company cars. Your lawyer or CPA cannot possibly know which combination of choices you and your partners would prefer from among the many sound possibilities in the structuring and programming of a corporation. If left to their own devices, they might set a course for your corporation that is too conservative and unimaginative and no better for you in sum than your unincorporated status. Or, they might simply make a choice in fringe benefits that does not suit you and your colleagues as much as another choice would have. Furthermore, if you are like most people, not understanding what is taking place would cause you to feel uneasy. You will feel much more comfortable with your corporation if you understand the important options and pick the ones you think best.

There is another point that is just as important — the looming presence of the IRS. If the officers and directors of your corporation are mere figureheads, IRS might very well label your corporation a partnership or proprietorship in fact and tax you accordingly. Despite the absolutely moral obligation every taxpayer owes himself to reduce his taxes to the legal minimum through any and all devices available, IRS has shown little tolerance for members of the professions who incorporate solely to avoid taxes. Such a frank reason might be all right for a businessman in the eyes of the IRS, but not all right for physicians, lawyers, dentists, and other licensed professionals.

Business corporations were well established by the time income taxes became law in 1913, and the tax collection machinery was relatively feeble until World War II. Otherwise, the federal tax collectors might have attacked business corporations as simply a tax dodge if they too had appeared as recently as the professional corporation. Internal Revenue Service fought the basic principle of professional corporations from 1948 until a series of defeats in the tax courts caused the IRS to throw in the towel in 1969. Then, while reserving the right to

challenge any individual corporation, they accepted the professional corporation concept and the floodgates were opened. In the meantime, individual states had been enacting special laws recognizing the rights of professionals to incorporate, and today all the states and the District of Columbia have such laws on their books. Nevertheless, not all losers are graceful, and it will take some time for IRS, still smarting from its setbacks, to stop holding professional corporations to narrow definitions of the law.

So the road to incorporation by professionals is now legally clear, though not entirely without potholes along the way and continuing after you get there. In the pages that follow, we intend to mark the biggest potholes while providing the travel plan that will indicate what and how to pack, what to look for (and look out for) along the way, what the route is, and what to expect once you get there.

The subject of incorporation can be almost as simple or as complicated as you choose to make it. The actual mechanics of becoming incorporated are simple, quick, and painless — made so partly by the forms in this book and models included in the appendix. Incorporation certainly is not quite so simple as buying a ticket and climbing on board. Nor is it necessarily so complicated as many authors and others lead one to believe. Too many well-qualified sources on the subject simply overwhelm and discourage the prospect in their earnest attempts to be helpful.

Our purpose in this book is to give you the subject in manageable bites. No one can learn all there is to know about corporations between the two covers of any book. But you surely can learn enough in reading this book to decide whether you and your colleagues should incorporate, what to consider before you do, how to go about it, and how to make it work for you. We also give you a form you can use in applying for incorporation in your state, reference numbers for the state corporation laws, and the addresses in each state to write for information and to submit your Articles of Incorporation.* You can use the form we provide, get one from your state if it provides them, or have an attorney draw one up for you. Whatever the case, the information in the book, along with the forms and models included to guide you, will enable you to draw up your own papers. If you are not an attorney yourself, you might prefer to have one do it for you. Remember though, that anyone can legally file incorporation papers without a lawyer. You do not have to use the special language of law, as long as you state clearly what, within the law, you want and do not want for your corporation. You could save a lot of money doing it yourself; some lawyers do charge fees in the thousands of dollars

for this relatively simple, well-defined step.

Your tax attorney or accountant can counsel you in the subtleties, help fill in the details, and answer your questions as you probe your way into the important decisions. Until you know what questions to ask, however, or what questions your counsel is likely to ask you, you're wasting money talking to expensive advisors. You can also go into the subject or any part of it as deeply as you wish, simply by turning to references in this bibliography and studying them in depth. You can become a real expert in your own right. But to do so is not necessary, nor even very common — especially among persons whose chosen occupation is not business. Keep in mind that the accumulation of money requires balance; if you work too hard at holding onto your money, you will be reducing your capacity to earn it in the first place. But the reverse is like trying to fill a bathtub with both the faucet and the drain wide open.

Your having read this far indicates that your drain might not be wide open, but you suspect it is leaking more than it should. As a logical starting point, let's run through the advantages and disadvantages of a corporation, how they apply to a professional practice, and how they might effect you.

* Also called Certificate of Incorporation. These terms are used interchangeably throughout this book.

Advantages of a Professional Corporation

The advantages (and disadvantages) of incorporation for a professional person are basically the same as for nonprofessionals. Before World War II, doctors, lawyers, engineers, and others, had no real reason to be interested in corporations. In the past three decades, however, growing taxation and changes in the tax laws, greater interference by government, increasing incomes, inflation, and accelerating complexity in general, have radically altered the status of the professions. As a result, there are now very sound business and professional reasons why many individuals and partnerships have converted to the corporate entity, and why many more right now are seriously considering the same for themselves.

The tax and retirement benefits are obviously the great motivators. Still, some of the seemingly lesser benefits can in the long run be of equal importance. Therefore, you should not consider the following list as necessarily in any order of priority any more than you should infer that it is a complete list. Moreover, the benefits will vary from person to person and from one time to another. Most of them, however, are valid for most professionals weighing the decision to incorporate.

Retirement Plan. This is probably the largest attraction for most persons. Even with the Keogh Plan*, which was instituted to provide professionals and others with the tax and retirement benefits afforded corporation employees, the latter still enjoy a decided advantage. If

---

* See Glossary of Terms

you have a Keogh Plan, you are well aware of its $7,500 or 15 percent of earnings limitation. The accumulation of such installments with other retirement benefits will provide a comfortable living (if inflation is controlled) for many individuals once they have stopped working. But for others who have enjoyed a high standard of living during their prime earning years, the limitations of the Keogh Plan would cause an abrupt shift in their living habits during retirement. Their Keogh, of course, could be supplemented by other investments designed to accumulate retirement funds. But such investments would be made with after-tax dollars and, with hardly any exception, the income from those investments would be taxed on a current basis. On the other hand, a qualified corporate retirement plan, without the Keogh limitations, is funded with before-tax dollars and can accumulate retirement funds without paying annual taxes. And a corporation offers other, related benefits:

Deferred Bonus or Salary Payments. This is a form of income-averaging, the point being to shift surplus income from high-income, high-tax years to low-income, low-tax retirement years. By deferring the bonuses or a portion of one's salary until retirement, a high-bracket individual shelters his most vulnerable income from taxation, ultimately paying a much lower tax on it and thereby saving substantial sums of money. Meanwhile, the surplus is available to the corporation for investment

on the employee's behalf and is also deductible to the corporation.

To make it strictly legitimate in the eyes of IRS, however, the corporation employee has to formally relinquish any control over the deferred income, the accumulated equity to be distributed by the corporation upon his retirement. Therefore, if the corporation should fail (as opposed to the voluntary dissolution of a successful corpoation), the deferred equity would be lost. Failure, however, even though it is a possibility for any venture, should not be as great a concern for a professional corporation as for a new business corporation, since most business failures are due to insufficient income and capital and to poor management.

Profit-sharing, Stock Options, Money-purchase, and Fixed-benefit Pension Plans. These are variations available under the classification of retirement benefits. Among professional corporations, profit-sharing and money-purchase plans are more common than a fixed-benefit pension plan for retired employees, largely because of their greater flexibility and potential for greater reward.

The fixed-benefit pension plan is favored by older employees because it can provide a more generous retirement and a fixed, predictable distribution rate based on an optional but predetermined formula (length of service, age, percentage of compensation, amount of fixed contribution, etc.). Unlike the profit-sharing or money-purchase type of plan, its funding is not limited by law, which means that a pension plan can accumulate a greater retirement fund over a shorter period of time. Its only limitation is at distribution. The Employee Retirement Income Security Act (ERISA) of the mid-seventies limits distribution at retirement to 100 percent of the average of the three best years or $80,745, whichever is lower. This was a recent escalation of the base rate, and it may be anticipated, however, that these escalators will continue over time.

A profit-sharing plan is limited by law to 15 percent of an employee's total compensation (up to 25 percent in any one year to raise the average to 15 percent), or up to 25 percent for any combination of profit-sharing and fixed-contribution plans. Voluntary contributions by an employee may be added to the corporate contributions but only up to 10 percent of the employee's salary. A profit-sharing plan has no age or service limitations placed upon it, is usually based on a ratio of each participating employee's compensation. Its ultimate benefit to an employee can be considerably greater than a fixed-benefit pension plan, especially to younger employees, although it can offer no guaranteed benefit level.

Still another type of retirement plan is the money-purchase plan, which is kind of a compromise between a profit-sharing and a pension plan. Like the profit-sharing plan, annual contri-butions are based on compensation, not on age or longevity, but are subject to the lesser of a 25 percent of compensation or $25,000* limit. Depending on how much within the limit is paid in, and for how long, the benefits at retirement are "whatever the money will purchase."

A point of primary concern for many professionals considering incorporation is the federal statute covering employee discrimination in retirement plans. The law says that a corporation may not provide disproportionate retirement benefits for one category of employee. But a perfectly legal way to reduce or eliminate corporate retirement contributions, other than F.I.C.A. contributions, for rank-and-file employees is to integrate the plan with Social Security. The integration process is fairly involved and depends on which kind of retirement plan(s) you use, but the principle for all of them is this: Every corporation is required to contribute a prescribed amount to the Social Security account of every employee. A corporation may also contribute to a supplementary fund for every employee. Formulas established by law, and allowing some latitude in choice of a formula to apply for all employees, establishes integration levels. Within a legal maximum, corporate contributions to the retirement plan can be at one percentage of salary below the integration level and a higher percentage above that level. In

---

*Plus on-going cost of living escalators, as provided for by ERISA.

principle, any employee can receive the higher percentage; but in practice, only the higher-paid professional employees qualify for it.

Regardless of the plan, a corporation has several built-in advantages over an individual who is saving for retirement: (1) Except for a Keogh plan or an Individual Retirement Account for employees not covered by a pension plan, all investments by an individual are made with after-tax dollars. The investments made for him by his corporation, on the other hand, are made with before-tax dollars. (2) A Keogh plan is restricted to the investment choices of the bank, trust, or insurance company selected to administer the plan and is limited to 15 percent or $7,500 of a person's income, an IRA to 15 percent or $1,750, whichever is less. Integration with Social Security, mentioned a moment ago, coupled with other features of a corporate plan, provides a more generous retirement income for the professional employees while costing the corporation less for the nonprofessional employees. (3) The usually larger purchasing power of a corporation can provide a buying leverage with flexibility of choice not available to the individual, either through selective investments or a mutual fund. (4) Option in deciding vested rights is a key advantage. The Keogh plan requires immediate vesting of all employees. A corporate plan can delay vesting for ten years, providing an incentive to new employees to stay with the corporation as they approach their tenth

anniversary. Anyone who leaves before then costs the corporation nothing, forfeiture working to the benefit of remaining employees. It's a form of deductible compensation and, like insurance, is much less expensive than the nondeductible kind. (5) Benefits can be paid to designated beneficiaries free of federal estate or gift tax.

These are some of the benefits of incorporation. There are many others, the principal ones including:

Insurance. As we said a moment ago, a corporation can buy more for the same amount of money or buy the same for less money. The amount saved depends on whether the corporation is in the 20 percent, the 22 percent, or the 48 percent income tax bracket — whether its taxable income is under $25,000 or over $50,000. But for the self-employed professional who pays for insurance with after-tax dollars, a corporation provides a substantial savings either way. Moreover, group life insurance is less expensive than the same amount purchased by an individual.

Term insurance vs. permanent. As with practically every other point of discussion, the subject of insurance has many facets that deserve consideration before laying down one's money. On all points, however, we intend to draw the discussion line after covering the principal features of the subject, lest in dwelling on the trees we lose sight of the woods. One aspect of the insurance woods you should file in your mind as important is the cost of term insurance versus whole or straight life. It is not, as some persons think, merely a matter of term insurance giving more disaster coverage for less money, but nothing back if there is no claim against it. As a matter of fact, whole life can be cheaper than term insurance for the same protection, depending on your tax situation. Insurance provided as a fringe benefit by your corporation is, of course, deductible to the corporation, whether it is term or whole life. (But the whole life premiums paid for you by the corporation are considered personal income by IRS.) For an individual or a corporation in a 48 percent tax bracket, the whole life policy that is financed (by borrowing against cash value to pay premiums) is cheaper over the long run because most of the payments beyond seven years go to interest, which is deductible. So don't overlook whole life in planning your insurance needs.

Tax-free insurance. Finally, of prime importance among insurance benefits from a corporate viewpoint is that up to $50,000 of life insurance can be provided to each employee tax free. This group term package must apply to all employees of the corporation, or to at least ten if there are more than ten employees. As in the case of retirement plans, the coverage must be nondiscriminatory. If coverage is not computed as a straight percentage of salary, coverage brackets are allowable but no bracket in a corporation of fewer than ten employees can offer more than two and a half

times the coverage of the next lower bracket, with the top bracket no more than ten times the coverage of the lowest. Also, a reasonable amount of life insurance can be obtained without a medical examination.

Section 79. The tax advantages described above are from Section 79 of the Internal Revenue Code. That code also makes possible the purchase of permanent life insurance at a substantially reduced total outlay for premiums. Even though the corporation cannot deduct the premiums for whole, or permanent, life insurance, it can call such payments on behalf of an employee additional compensation, which is deductible. The employee, of course, pays income tax on the additional compensation; but the corporate deductions and the tax benefits under Section 79 for the diminishing term portion of the policy add up to net shareholder-employee savings on permanent life that are impressive.

Split-dollar insurance. A variation on the funding of permanent life insurance for the individual shareholder-employee is handled through a split-dollar arrangement. Under this method, the corporation pays for that portion of premiums representing the cash value, and the employee pays for the portion representing the term coverage. As the cash value increases, therefore, the employee's payments decrease to a point at which he is paying nothing. The corporation is the beneficiary for the cash value in the event of the employee's death, the employee's beneficiary receiving the difference between the cash value and the face value of the policy. To offset the declining death benefit for the employee's beneficiary, the corporation buys additional term insurance for the employee out of the cash dividends. The net effect of split-dollar insurance is increased whole life coverage for key people at greatly reduced cost.

Workman's Compensation. This important benefit is not available to the self-employed person but most definitely is to employees of a corporation. And its benefits are not limited to wage-roll employees, either. It is available to every employee of a corporation, from the president on down, but it does not have to include all employees. And its benefits are not limited to accidents incurred at work, as many persons mistakenly believe. Disability benefits include compensation for permanent disability, and death benefits to survivors, including a $5,000 tax-free payment. With limitations, benefits are all tax free, and the cost is a tax deduction for the corporation.

Health Insurance and Medical Payments. Members of the medical and pharmaceutical professions enjoy a reciprocity with each other that substantially reduces medical costs, but does not eliminate them altogether. In some instances also, individual members of different professions have informally associated with each other to trade professional services. Nevertheless, al-most everyone has medical and dental expenses, and for most individuals only a fraction of those expenses is deductible, if anything. The higher one's income, in fact, the less likely are medical expenses to exceed the 1 percent and 3 percent of income that is not deductible. Under a medical reimbursement plan, however, a corporation can deduct the full cost of medical payments made to employees and their families as a fringe benefit, and the employees do not have to pay taxes on the payments as income.

Profit Accumulation. The law allows a corporation to accumulate profits to a reasonable limit to cover operating expenses and contingencies. The outside limit is $150,000 over the life of the corporation — a fairly sizable sum of sheltered income, especially for a small corporation. Beyond that limit, the tax bite becomes vicious, making it desirable for the corporation to reinvest additional profits in capital improvements or else distribute them as dividends.

Lower Corporate Tax Rates. The licensed professional in a 50 percent tax bracket will appreciate the advantage of letting his corporation take some of his income as profit and pay only 20 percent if the corporation's profit for the year is not more than $25,000. Profits above that are taxed at 22 percent and at 48 percent above $50,000. Besides, profits invested by the corporation in other corporations get a three-way benefit with which you almost can't lose:

Dividend Exemption. If your corporation's stock in other corporations appreciates, like an individual it pays the lower capital gains tax and only when it sells the stock. If the stock value falls, your corporation can offset profits to the extent of the loss, thereby reducing its taxes. And any dividends from the stock are tax-free income for your corporation, up to 85 percent of the dividends. For a corporation paying 20 percent on its profits, the remaining nonexempt 15 percent of dividends received is taxed at a real rate of about 3 percent.

Tax Option on Losses. Since business losses for a corporation shelter its income against tax rates of only 20 percent to 48 percent, shareholders with outside income they would like to shelter might cast covetous glances at any of the corporation's losses. Under Subchapter S, a qualifying corporation can pass its operating losses — but not its capital losses — directly to shareholders to apply as a deduction against personal income. Subchapter S is an option that must be exercised and adhered to formally, however, and not on the opportunity of the moment. It is a feature of corporation tax law designed to accomodate the small businessman in his corporate status, so that he can enjoy benefits both of incorporation and self-employment. Its benefits to shareholders in a professional corporation, however, are dubious. First of all, a professional corporation is not likely to suffer operating losses; secondly, the doubtful benefits would be offset by the loss of substantial benefits mentioned above; and finally, except for outside income, personal income from the professional corporation can be adjusted to the best balance between corporate taxes and personal income taxes (providing, of course, the IRS considers the adjustments reasonable). Our main purpose in mentioning Subchapter S is the question that omitting discussion of it might raise among readers of this book.

There is another way of having your cake and eating it too, and it is called Section 1244 stock. If you register your stock as Section 1244 when you incorporate, the stock can be deducted from gross personal income as an ordinary — not just a capital — loss, should it ever become depressed or worthless. Since there are no disadvantages in 1244 stock, every corporation should take advantage of it even though its shareholders will probably never have to exercise the advantage.*

Fiscal Year Flexibility. A self-employed person pays his income tax on a calendar year. So may a corporation. But a corporation may also elect to pay taxes

---

* Complete instructions for registering stock under Section 1244 are included in the Corporate Kit supplied by the Professional Corporation Co. See page 121.

on any fiscal year of its choosing. Professions of a seasonal or other cyclical nature might gain some investment or tax advantage by timing their fiscal year in accordance with the ebb and flow of income. If at no other time, there might be a one-shot benefit in converting a proprietorship or partnership to a fiscal-year corporation, thereby concentrating or spreading one's income for a net reduction in taxes.

Other Than Tax Advantages. So far, the advantages we have listed involve taxes and the manifestations of tax savings. The summary comment on that important aspect of incorporation is the long-term appreciation of your professional corporation and the low-tax capital gain to you when you surrender (as you must) your stock in the corporation at full retirement. Added to your retirement income from the corporation, plus social security and any other income you might have, you could be six digits ahead of your alternate retirement position without the corporate benefits.

And we haven't even finished listing the benefits — important ones even though not directly related to income and taxes. Before we go on, though, we would be remiss in not reiterating that there are drawbacks and disadvantages for some people in following the corporate route. We will get to them after we discuss briefly some more advantages that should enter into your deliberations about incorporating.

Limited Liability. For businessmen, this is often the most important benefit in a corporation. The shareholder is liable only to the extent of his investment, whereas a sole proprietor or a partner is legally liable for the entire business, whether or not he is personally culpable.

The liability status of the shareholder in a professional corporation, however, is neither so limited nor yet so well defined. The problem involves business versus professional liability and where to draw the line of departure between the two. As a general rule, state laws governing professional corporations specifically enunciate the traditional ethical relationship between the professional and his patient or client, thereby retaining through law all the privileges and liabilities of that relationship. The shareholder in a professional corporation, then, is personally liable for the professional service he renders and for any service performed by a subordinate under his direction. So, too, is the corporation liable since, technically, it is the corporation providing the service through its professionally-licensed employees. We mention this, not because otherwise some physician might think he could escape malpractice suits through incorporation, but to point out one of the peculiarities of the professional corporation as opposed to the business corporation. It was this point as much as any other, in fact, that impeded the development of professional corporations, serving effectively as an ulterior argument of the IRS in its war against this entity.

Several states, nevertheless, have tried to be fair to the licensed professional by granting him the same legal protection as any other corporate shareholder in any matters involving nonprofessional transactions. After all, a professional corporation is regularly involved with investments, contracts, construction, transportation, communication and other activities of human intercourse that could involve liability having nothing to do with the profession. So it seems only fair in these matters to grant the same legal protection to professionals as to other people, and the courts would likely agree.

Centralized Management. The very disciplines required of a corporation tend to give it an efficiency of operation and an edge in productivity and economy over the same practice run as a partnership or a self-employed individual. The efficiency is not automatic, however, and the required discipline and formalities of a professional corporation are to some persons a drawback rather than an asset.

Easy Transfer of Ownership. Removing oneself from an ownership role is merely a matter of selling one's shares to another qualified person or to the corporation itself. The method of ownership transfer and of figuring the value of a share will have already been established in the articles of incorporation, and agreed to in advance by the shareholders

and directors; so there should be no delay over these matters. A one-man corporation might find the transfer of ownership more akin to liquidating a proprietorship, but in general a corporation smoothes out transition of ownership. Particularly in the event of unexpected death, a corporation can protect the shareholder's survivors from the rigors of liquidation under unfavorable circumstances. Conversely, survival of the business is better assured through the corporate from if a key person dies suddenly.

Raising Capital. Usually a corporation can raise more capital and do it easier than one or several persons can. An obvious reason is the shares of stock a corporation exchanges for invested funds (professional corporations, however, can sell shares only to a person licensed by the state to practice the same profession as the corporation) but another is the implied efficiency mentioned above. It must be admitted, though, that sometimes creditors will require the principals of a new corporation to sign personal guarantees, simply because of the limited liability of a shareholder.

Coping With Complexity. Even though there will always be one-man professional practices, and with valid reasons for the persons involved, the trend among professional men has been toward group practice. This is largely a phenomenon of the increasing complexity of our society and of a human inability to be expert in all aspects of a discipline. Group practice can bring together a variety of talents and specialties into one responsible entity. As a corporation — legally a single person — the group of specialists once again resumes, in a way, the aspect of the general practitioner or family doctor of yesteryear but with the technical breadth and depth required today. A group never attains the integration of an individual, of course, but a group can be a happy compromise between the necessarily limited individual and the many scattered, detached specialists. The group can even take on a "personality" that is distinct from any one of its members.

Professional people, however, are often individualistic by nature, which in group practice can be as much a liability as an asset. It is unusual to find real compatibility between two persons, and the problem is compounded in mathematical progression as additional persons join a group. The trend toward group practice is a reflection of compromise between individual inclinations on the one hand and individual benefits from associated endeavor on the other hand. By benefits we mean the sharing of overhead, a reduction of pressure, easier consultation with peers, greater flexibility in the personal use of one's time, more efficiency, and greater earning power, among others. All these considerations can be present in a partnership, to be sure, but a corporation has one inherent advantage over a partnership: It is a government of law, not men. It tends to insulate against interpersonal friction in the regular conduct of the practice. Every shareholder has a say in the formulation of the corporate laws, and incidental differences are more easily resolved by reference to those laws, or bylaws. A clash of willpowers in fruitless argument is less likely to occur.

Another important consideration lies in the recruitment of new talent to work with or for the group. It is critical to the vitality and longevity of the practice. Yet government and business are taking a growing share of professional graduates who are lured by the security and the competitive advantages of broad fringe benefits. In order to compete for the best talent, therefore, a group of professional consultants or practitioners must offer security, prestige, and compensation that compare favorably with that of the competition. A professional corporation, run in an efficient, business-like manner, having an excellent reputation in the profession and the community, and offering equal benefits and perhaps greater potential for the prospective employee, has it all over a partnership.

Regular Paychecks and Tax Withholding. Many professionals look upon these two attributes of corporate employment as refreshing new benefits. Their personal finances are simplified by a predictable paycheck, as well as by the elimination of their quarterly tax estimates. They consider them benefits even though technically, at least, they are losing investment income on the taxes paid prematurely.

Disadvantages of a Professional Corporation

Nothing is perfect, and that certainly goes for corporations as it does for proprietorships and partnerships. We do believe that the assets of a corporation outweigh the liabilities, and as a general observation we feel that is true whether we are discussing a business or a profession, a one- or two- or many-person operation. But a corporation is not for everyone, for the following main reasons:

Initial Cost. As with anything else, there are expensive ways to do things, and there are inexpensive ways to do the same things. You can spend several thousand dollars with a lawyer and several thousand more with an accountant getting a corporation organized, or you can spend a few hundred dollars altogether getting your corporation launched. One of the leading corporation agencies in the world — The Company Corporation, founded by this writer and headquartered at 1300 Market Street in Wilmington, Delaware — has helped thousands of business corporations get started at a total cost of incorporation of less than fifty dollars. This writer has also founded a corporation agency to help professional corporations. It is called the Professional Corporation Co. Detailed information about this company will be covered later in this book.

Not many attorneys or accountants will tell you that you don't need them, for indeed they can be helpful — even necessary if you do not get the needed information otherwise. The responsibility is yours, and the more you learn before approaching professional help, the less you will have to pay for it. One point should be made right here: There is no legal requirement that you be represented by a lawyer in forming a corporation. You could use a form right in the back of this book and complete it yourself. Most professional persons already have an attorney if not also an accountant, and they will continue to have them after they have formed a corporation. If their services are used, only that portion of them spent specifically on forming and running the corporation should figure in the extra cost of incorporating.

As a corporation you will have to maintain records and make reports not required of a less formal entity. Every corporation has to file an income tax report, which means two reports for a one-man corporation. And a professional corporation particularly has to conduct its affairs in a thorough, efficient, and formal manner. This takes more time and somewhat more money than other entities might require. But in the long run it is usually a good investment, for reasons we have already mentioned.

Paperwork. Some persons detest so much the simplest details, such as keeping corporate minutes, they would rather pay for the luxury of avoiding them. Even if you pay other persons to handle the details, some of them are unavoidable — and for some persons, unthinkable. This type of person probably should forget about incorporating.

Double Taxation. Shareholders in a corporation may get hit twice — actually thrice: The corporation pays taxes on its profits, the shareholder-employee pays taxes on his salary from the corporate income not taxed, and also pays taxes on any corporate profits distributed to him as dividends. He also usually pays state and often local taxes on the same gross income, even though there is deductible reciprocity. Multilayered taxation is common for any taxable income; it is just more so with corporations.

Management Flexibility. Corporations offer greater tax flexibility; but on paper, at least, they are more rigid and ponderous when it comes to changing policies. An individual or several partners can decide on a change and do it. But with a corporation a quorum of directors must vote on a policy matter not covered in the articles or bylaws, and technically the decision must be formally recorded before the policy can be implemented. The meeting can be conducted by telephone, provided this option is mentioned in the bylaws, and the matter might take no more actual effort than would be required without a corporation. Psychologically, if not actually, the procedure is more cumbersome, however.

Lack of Privacy. Corporations are governed by state laws, and there are differences from one state to another, although there are remarkable similarities too. A prevalent similarity is the requirement for filing annual reports. A corporation whose stock is traded on the market must invariably report all its financial details, including the compensation of its officers. This is in fact a requirement of the Securities and Exchange Commission of the federal government. But even a close corporation, one whose stock is closely held by one or a few persons and not publicly offered for sale, must file an annual report to the state in which it is chartered. The report usually has to contain the names and addresses of shareholders, directors, and officers, along with other information, and generally takes only a few minutes to complete. It is available for any legitimate examination by outsiders. This makes semipublic the kind of confidential information you might prefer to keep confidential, even at the cost of foregoing substantial benefits from incorporation.

Tax Audits. The IRS may be more likely to audit a professional corporation than a staff or self-employed professional, and the corporation audit will lead to an audit of its shareholder-employees. So a professional who prides himself on never having been audited (a luxury, perhaps, purchased at the cost of higher-than-necessary taxes paid) could be in for an unenjoyable experience. We must ask, however, what price one is willing to pay for serenity. To answer in the ridiculous to make a point, we could suggest that everyone file the short Form 1040 with standard deduction. It would be very expensive, but it would guarantee freedom from tax audits.

The Special Aspects of a Professional Corporation

The explicit definition of a professional corporation in every state law on the subject is a corporation organized to provide any professional service for which a license or other authority issued by the state is prerequisite to rendering the service. To clarify the point, some statutes go on to list many of the professions that would fall under the definition, while stating that the law is not confined to the professions listed. If the records were examined, they would show literally every known profession represented by the corporate form. But a good guess would place medicine at the top of the list numerically. If so, dentistry, accounting, engineering, and law, are numerically well represented also.

In the appendix to this book we have listed the reference number for the professional corporation law in each state and the District of Columbia. With each reference you will also find an address so you can request specific information from the jurisdiction in which your corporation would be chartered. The information in this chapter is a compendium of all states and presents a generally accurate picture of the main differences between a professional corporation and a business corporation. One general observation emerges from a study of all state laws on the subject, and that is the repetition — in many instances word for word — from one state law to another. Some states are very thorough in response to requests for information; others are slow, incomplete, grudging, or even unresponsive without prodding. But in virtually all states certain features exist, either by written statute or precedent in practice, regarding the formation and operation of professional corporations. The principal rules and exceptions follow:

Professional Corporation Identification. Most states lump all professions together under one statute, and that statute lists the particular requirements and limitations imposed on a corporation by its professional status. Any item not covered by the professional corporation law is covered by the general (business) corporation law. Several states have a different statute for each major profession. Some qualify medicine under one law, all other professions under another. Some states refer to them as "professional corporations," some call them "professional service corporations," others, "professional associations." Some states require the word "limited" or its abbreviation, or "chartered" or "incorporated." Others will not allow use of the words "incorporated," or "company," or their abbreviations. Most states do require that the corporate name be followed by the designated professional corporation term or its abbreviation, although they also permit a short form to be used in daily matters, including the dropping of the corporate identification.

Corporate Name. On the subject of names, most states follow the traditional practice of using the last names of principal members, probably because it gives the corporation a sharper identity as well as also implying the professional nature of the corporation. Some states are pretty rigid about that requirement, in which cases a discussion of pros and cons is academic. The name of the corporation can be very important, however, and persons in states that allow a choice should think about the following:

Use of Last Names. Typically professional, more personal, less likely to be a duplication of another corporation and therefore unallowed. Some names not very euphonic, too many can be cumbersome if not ludicrous, but which should be excluded? Delete names as principals retire, add names of new principals? Very expensive and confusing to be always changing the name of the corporation, less chance to build recognition and confidence in it. But keeping the original name eventually would signify nothing of specific identity.

Assumed Name. Can be descriptive of the corporation's specialty. Allows continuity regardless of personnel changes. Can be shorter, more easily remembered and used. It might have a more businesslike sound to it. But: To many patients and clients, the intimate personal relationship is a necessity; they might consider a nonpersonal name too cold and indifferent and also an indication that they might not get to deal with the professional of their choice.

Whatever your ultimate choice in names, it will be checked for duplication against other company names doing business in the state or reserved for that purpose. There is usually a $5 fee charged by the state for running the check and reserving a name for a specified period of time.

General Corporation Law. Every state recognizes the professional corporation to be a fully bonafide corporation — a corporate "person" qualified to own property, to invest money, to sue and be sued, to have perpetual existence if desired, to employ help, to sell products and services and to collect for them, to form trusts, to make and receive loans, to provide for its own dissolution, and to do whatever else corporations do by law and by custom in the process of making a profit.

Exception. The chapters of state law dealing with professional corporations were written because the general corporation laws did not stipulate the necessary areas of departure from business corporations required of professional corporations to protect the public and the respective professions. Any conflicts between the general corporation law and the professional corporation law regarding a professional corporation are always resolved in favor of the latter.

Limited Activity. Not limited in degree but in kind. A business corporation deliberately describes its purpose in a very general way so as not to restrict its opportunities. A professional corporation *must* by law limit its activities to the practice of its specified profession. It can engage in no other business, only in such activities as support the investment programs of the corporation and its necessary business functions.

Exception. A number of states permit a professional corporation to provide the services of two or more specifically related professions, such as engineering, surveying and architecture. The employees of the corporation rendering service in a specific profession, however, must be licensed by the state to perform that service.

Registered Agent. Because business corporations often operate in states outside their home state, or the corporation's owners do not live in the state in which the company is incorporated, states require a corporation that is doing business in the state to have a legal mailing address and personal agent located in the county of principal office in that state and registered with the secretary of state's office (and sometimes with the county clerk as well). The agent can be the corporation itself if it is physically located in the state, or it can be a legal resident or another corporation in the state empowered to act as a registered agent.

For a professional corporation this standard device for giving states a handle on foreign-source activities is more or less academic. Since its practicing employees must all be licensed in the state of incorporation, they and the corporation are most likely to be physically located there too.

Many professional and business corporations maintain a registered agent in the state in which they both incorporate and practice, even though they are not legally required to do so. Reasons for this include the help the agent can give them in forming the corporation; qualifying the corporation to function in any other state; assistance in filing annual reports; the forwarding of legal mail to and from the secretary of state; and handling process of service, which means the receipt and forwarding of any legal papers such as would be involved in prosecuting or defending a lawsuit. Furthermore, it is often a good idea to maintain a permanent legal address in your state because professional offices seem to relocate a surprising number of times over the years. Costs for a registered agent vary. The annual fee charged by Professional Corporation Co. for most states is only $50 a year. One feature of the service is a bulletin containing helpful suggestions on taxes and other matters of interest to the professional corporation.

For these reasons, most professional corporations would benefit by maintaining a registered agent in the state in which the practice is based, as well as in any other state in which the corporation practices.

It would not be unprecedented for a professional or a group of them to be incorporated in a state having more favorable corporation laws, but practicing in their home state. They would have to maintain license in both states, of course. For example, a Pennsylvania physician, licensed to practice in both Pennsylvania and Delaware, might incorporate in Delaware because of its attractive corporation law, while maintaining his home, office and practice in Pennsylvania for patients of both states. In such a case, then, he would appoint a registered Delaware agent to comply with the state's demand for a local agent and address.

Mergers. Most laws allow the merger of two corporations providing the same professional services. Some states permit a domestic (chartered in that state) professional corporation to merge with a foreign (chartered in another state) corporation of the same profession, provided that the merged corporation performs services in the profession only through employees who are licensed to practice that profession in the state. Several states — Oregon, for example — do not allow foreign professional corporations to practice in the state at all, even through employees licensed to practice the profession in Oregon. The importance of a state's recognition of mergers and foreign professional corporations is apparent in those population centers of the country located near the border of two or more states. Any professional corporation that would maintain separate facilities in different parts of the metropolitan area for the convenience of its patients or clients (and thus the growth of the practice) might be thwarted by a law in any of the states that did not allow foreign professional corporations to practice. The only solution to such a problem might be to establish the home office in the restrictive state and the branches in the adjacent state.

The Stock. There is no limit to the numbers of shares a professional corporation may issue or the amount of paid-in capital. Several states require that a specified minimum (such as $1,000) be provided. They can be voting or non-voting shares, can have a par value or no par value.* Most corporations today choose the latter since par value has little if any meaning, and in the case of one state, the filing fee for no par stock is half as much as for stock with a stated par value. It will also be common stock* — a legal requirement in many states.

The shares of a professional corporation in virtually all states can be held only by the corporation or by a person licensed by that state to perform the specified professional service. An employee-shareholder who stops practicing in the state, retires from practice, or loses his license to practice, must, within a prescribed time limit, sell his shares to another person licensed in the profession or to the corporation. The survivors or estate of a shareholder who dies must likewise sell his shares. Besides being spelled out in detail in many of the laws, the bylaws of a corporation should also state the procedure for transferring the ownership of stock. (See sample bylaws in the Appendix.)

Incorporators, Directors, Officers. Almost all states require only one

incorporator, although there may be any number. Some states require two incorporators, or three, as a minimum. Most require only one shareholder, who must be licensed in the profession and who must be the president and sometimes also the treasurer or secretary and a director of the corporation. In most states the other officers and the directors do not have to be licensed in the profession or shareholders in the corporation. But they may not participate in any activities or policy decisions involving the profession. To accommodate the professional in solo practice who wants to keep it that way but become incorporated, most of the states have made it possible for one man to incorporate and to operate by himself or with one other, not necessarily licensed, person (spouse, relative, or friend). Other states enable a professional corporation to operate with one licensed professional but require the corporation to have several directors, obviously as a precaution against mismanagement or poor business judgment.

Despite the legal blessings of the states on one-man professional corporations, the IRS includes them among their favorite targets for close scrutiny. We will discuss the problem in the next chapter.

State Regulating Boards. The state laws regularly defer to the state boards regulating the respective professions, in effect saying that the final judge and arbiter of

---

* See Glossary of Terms

ethical and professional policy will be the regulating or examining board. In many states the naming of corporations, the setting of certain fees, the qualifications of shareholder-employees, the articles of incorporation, and the annual reports of professional corporations must be presented to the state board for their approval before the secretary of state will issue a charter or a certificate of authority.

All the laws further say that nothing in the law is to interfere with the normal relationship between the regulating boards and the members of their respective professions, including the boards' responsibilities for disciplinary actions, the setting of standards, ethical conduct, and so forth. The laws also insure that nothing in the law will interfere with the professional relationship between a person rendering professional service and his patient or client, including privileged communications and professional liability.

Equitable Law. Even though the details differ from state to state, the intent of all states is to protect all interests in matters pertaining to professional services. The rights of the professions and their individual members, the rights of individuals who require the professional services, and the rights or interests of government have long been acknowledged in practice and law. It has only been in recent years, however, that the rights of professional men and women regarding equal taxation have been established in law. This book was written to help the professionals realize the benefits that are not generally available to them. Whether you, personally, elect to take the corporation route will depend on what kind of picture you see when you mentally put all the pieces together. The next chapter should further help you weigh some of the factors.

Should *You* Form A Professional Corporation?

That, of course, is a rhetorical question. The author certainly cannot answer it for you, and at this point you probably cannot answer it for yourself, either. At some point, however, you will answer it, for even making no decision is a form of making a decision. In any event, the odds say that sooner or later you will decide to incorporate.

If you do, what prompts you will not be just logic and facts that cause you to do it. It will be that, mixed with psychology and emotion. The decision might come right after a tax audit or simply after making out your income tax some year. Or it might happen after a classmate you considered likeable but not very capable takes you for a cruise on his new 50-footer. Or yet again when you see the sad situation of an older colleague whose retirement is little better than hand-to-mouth. It happens to many persons when they hit age 30 or 40 or 50. And once in a while it occurs when a person leaves someone else's employment and starts working for himself. There is a world of difference between the withheld income taxes that you never actually see and the beautiful cash-money-crinkly-green you work so hard to get but have to count out of your hand and into the tax collector's. That is when a body starts getting serious thoughts about taking less cash from his wallet to lay into the hand of IRS. One possible and legal way to do it is through incorporation.

Another point that is consistently overlooked, even though it is obvious and has been made many times already, is the inexorable ravage of inflation. Engineers smugly comment that they are making three times as much money as when they were hired ten years ago —

twice as much as when they started five years ago. Those are occupation averages, in fact. Engineers out of school ten years averaged $1,867 a month in 1975; out of school five years, they averaged $1,477 a month. Those figures are 293 percent and 169 percent, respectively, of the averages for 1965 and 1970. They have made a good gain but not as good as some of them believe. They are talking about numbers, not buying-power. Those are gross figures, remember, and taxes have doubled in ten years, too. The man who is making twice as much as in 1966 has progressed not at all, since today's dollar is worth less than a 1966 half dollar. On top of that, nearly every time he gets a raise he goes into a higher tax bracket, so he actually is losing ground. The median income for a general practitioner in 1974 was just over $40,000; specialists made more — certified family practitioners over $7,000 more. Physicians have been the butt of many jokes about their high income; but one seldom hears sympathy for the 40 percent they might pay on their taxable income or how much money, time and energy they invested in education, or the slave wages they received during their internship. Admittedly, though, no matter how you slice it, that's a lot of money — especially if the law says you do not have to give so much of it away.

Some of the questions and answers about incorporation are easy, because they involve facts. The hard questions to answer, and in the final analysis the most important ones, are those that are subjective.

Question: Can a corporation reduce taxes and increase net income?

Answer: Yes, it can.

Question: Does it cost a lot of money to form and operate a corporation?

Answer: It doesn't have to. Perhaps only a hundred dollars to start and less than a hundred extra a year to run. Besides, the net savings should easily offset the cost many times over.

Question: But isn't it true that you get what you pay for? Couldn't a skimping on expensive advice be very costly in the long run?

Answer: That maxim is often true, and it could be true for this subject too. What we are talking about is the *difference* between what you would spend for technical advice anyhow and how much more you might spend above that if you incorporate. Your accountant will help you with your taxes anyway. Your insurance man will advise you on the various kinds of insurance and what they can do. Your attorney will draft contracts and letters for you, help you settle disputes no matter how you are organized. It is in taking advantage of the unique opportunities a corporation offers in taxes, investments, retirement, and estate planning that your regular advisors will have to adjust what you already have, keep records of items that were unimportant before, and plan some entirely new projects. If your present advisors are not knowledgeable about corporations, they could be very costly indeed, but probably more costly in opportunities missed than in outright deficits.

Question: Isn't all the formality and red tape a pain in the neck?

Answer: Yes it is. But once you have sorted out the options and have made your choices, there isn't much more involvement than filling out an application for a job or a bank loan. The forms are already available to cover practically any action you might have to take or want to take. You'll find in the appendix of this book the basic forms and information about where to get the other things you want. We will discuss those items in the next chapter. Fill out the forms and file them with the designated authority. You can keep a checklist or a tickler system as a reminder of things that need doing as you go along, or you can leave that to one of your advisors or employees. You will have to participate actively in some matters, however.

Question: Could I get myself into some kind of horrible mess with a corporation that I wouldn't if I stayed away from incorporating?

Answer: You can die eating steak. The local, state and federal governments, your professional regulating board, your advisors, colleagues and friends, and your own reading and general awareness make a formidable combination against disaster. There are just too many trouble-shooting checkpoints built into the system. In addition, you have intelligence, education, a healthy market for your service, established income and credit, a good reputation, and a desire to succeed. Men have become legends of success in their own time with less on their side than that.

Question: I read somewhere that a doctor shouldn't think about incorporating unless he is grossing about $90,000. Another source said the rule-of-thumb is the 50 percent tax bracket. What's the truth?

Answer: They are both right and both wrong. For some doctors, $90,000 isn't nearly enough reason for them to incorporate. For others, a third of that is ample. There are just too many variables that can make a difference for anyone to apply magic formulas. You have to look at a person's balance sheet, spending and saving habits, attention to details, mode and standard of living, age, size of family, profile of his practice, long-range objectives, even his philosophy of life. If he has partners, you have to consider the same points for them and how all the parts fit together. A better rule-of-thumb would be the percentage of a person's income that goes for current spending. Almost no income is large enough to justify incorporating if the person receiving it has to spend it all as fast as it comes in. It takes money to make money or to save it. You need seed money of your own or from the bank, and you need a cushion of operating capital plus a surplus for the investments and capital accumulation that are the *raison d'etre* of a corporation. But the money itself is not the issue. The issue is your attitude and your present circumstances. If these are favorable, the seed money will be available and the rest will follow.

Question: I can see more sense in a group going together in a corporation than in one person doing it. Does a one-man practice really gain anything from incorporating?

Answer: The principles are the same for one person as for a group. A group has some natural advantages of pooling talents and workload, but the corporation cannot take much credit for that. The benefits of incorporation are there for singles as well as for multiples. Perhaps the biggest difference is the negative potential of not being accepted as a corporation for tax purposes; and without that you might as well not bother. The possible trouble — and it is only an outside possibility — lies in a label that reads "personal holding company." It is a subject of considerable importance for small corporations and deserving of discussion at some length right here:

The Personal Holding Company Problem. It should no longer be a problem, since at least one tax court has settled the issue in favor of the taxpayer. But as we said, the IRS dies hard. And if they ever got their way in this matter, the defendant could be bludgeoned with a tax bill from the highest bracket — 70 percent — regardless of the sum involved. In order to avoid it, you have to know what it is, however.

By definition, a personal holding company is one having, for the last half of a taxable year, more than half the value of its stock owned by fewer than six stockholders and receiving at least 60 percent of its income from "personal holding company income." By this they mean "passive" income from such sources as interest, dividends, rentals and capital gains -- income, in other words, that comes from capital investment; and they mean also income from personal service contracts. This is defined as service for which the person receiving the service designates the person who will perform it. If you feel hemmed in by the definition, don't close the book yet. Small professional corporations live despite this problem, and here's how:

Passive income from investments is a necessary fact of life, but it isn't likely to make up 60 percent of your corporation's income ever. The key to the situation lies in the matter of "personal contract" service. If your patient says, "I want you, Dr. Jones, to perform the root canal," and you reply, "All right, Mrs. Smith, you're the boss!" then theoretically you could have a problem if you handle every patient the same way. First of all, you have an employment contract with your corporation (that's right, even if you and your corporation are really one and the same, technically you're not) that clearly states the prerogative and necessity of the corporation to assign the duties and services of

the employee. Your corporation bylaws also state that the corporation has the sole responsibility for service assignments and also state that, during periods of your absence, the services of the corporation will be assigned by the corporation to certain other licensed members of the profession. It would be wise to further post such a statement in your waiting room. All this might seem to be technical subterfuge, but issues of law are often decided on technicalities — this specific issue included.

Looking at the matter realistically, experience has shown that, if all other attributes of a corporation are in line with precedent and the law, the corporation will not be challenged by the IRS simply because of its small size. Any IRS questions on this point are almost invariably tandem to questions on other points of the tax code.

How It Looks On Paper. Assuming that you are still interested and would like to see a more graphic comparison between the incorporated versus the unincorporated status for the same person, here is an overly simple, artificial but fairly typical case: Jonas J. Jones, M.D. (fictitious), age 42, married and with two dependent children, solo practice, net income from practice: $50,000. He pays $3,000 in life insurance premiums, $1,000 in health insurance premiums, $7,500 for his Keogh plan contribution, $6,000 in nonbusiness deductions, files a joint return.

Self-employed

Net Income		$50,000
Deduct Keogh Contribution	$ 7,500	
Itemized Deductions	6,000	
Exemptions (4 x $750)	3,000	
		−16,500
Taxable Income		$33,500
Federal Income Taxes (rate in a recent tax year)		9,290

Professional Corporation

Corporation Net Income		$50,000
Deduct Jones's Salary	$35,500	
Deduct Retirement Plan Contribution	10,500	
Deduct Life & Health Insurance Premiums	4,000	
		−50,000
Corporation Taxable Income		0

Jones's Salary		$35,500
Itemized Deductions	$ 6,000	
Exemptions	3,000	
		− 9,000
Taxable Income		$26,500
Federal Income Tax (1975 Rates)		$ 6,560

As you can see in this arbitrary and unrealistically simple — but valid — example, the corporation would save Dr. Jones $2,730 in taxes for the example year. That is surely much more than enough to pay the costs of planning, organizing and operating a corporation for its first year. Furthermore, the example does not include income from investments and the removal from taxation of corporate dividend income and accumulated profits.

Now let's look at it another way: How much spendable income is left after all expenses have been met as an individual and as a corporation.

Self-employed

Net Income		$50,000
Less Keogh Plan Contribution	$7,500	
Less Itemized Deductions	6,000	
Less Federal Income Taxes	9,290	
Less Life & Health Insurance Premiums	4,000	
		−26,790
Spendable Income		$23,210

Professional Corporation

Jones's Salary		$35,500
Less Federal Income Taxes	$6,560	
Less Itemized Deductions	6,000	
		−12,560
Spendable Income		$22,940

You might question whether itemized deductions should be subtracted any more than other, nondeductible expenses, including that part of any medical deduc- tions that cannot be itemized. Neverthe- less, the principle remains: Dr. Jones would have $270 more pocket money if self-employed, but that is because he is building a larger retirement nest egg through his corporation. Based on 8 percent interest compounded a year, at retirement age 65, Dr. Jones would have:

Keogh Plan: $432,344

Corporate Plan: $605,281

The corporation delivers $172,937 more over the twenty-two years in the retirement plan alone.

In the examples shown, the differences between the two entities in taxes, in spendable income, and in retirement capital are not necessarily projectable in the same ratios to all situations. Nevertheless, one can generally assume that a given income will produce a larger retirement fund over a specified time period and will pay lower taxes but produce less current income through a corporation than through an unincorporated practice.

In the pages following, we have provided worksheets to enable you to apply this information to your own particular situation.

Allocating Income. Incomes are not fixed, of course, and the needs of individuals change also. Young people usually need more current income during their family-building years than after their children leave home to start their own careers. That is why young people often put off such important matters as incorporating the practice; they need every cent they can scrape up to meet their personal commitments. It is the old story: You could save time if you had the time to get better organized; you could make more money and save more

if you could just get a little more money so you could buy more efficiently, expand your base or make some investments.

One advantage of a corporation in line with this too-common problem is the flexibility of compensation. As a decision-maker at the same time you are an employee, you can favor either salaries or corporate investments, within reason and subject to IRS approval. You can pay yourself a relatively higher salary in the early years when you need income and then shift your income weight toward the retirement plan and other investments when your current needs are met and your interest shifts toward thoughts of the "golden years." We will cover some additional points regarding income allocation in the next chapter.

Financial Help. If, as a result of current needs, you have not been able to get together the capital for starting your own practice — in any form — you might very well get help from a bank or the Small Business Administration, or both. Loan policies and decisions vary from one loan officer to another, from bank to bank, from one part of the country to another and from one time to another with the same lender. You might safely assume, however, that if you have half the capital you need to get started, some bank will take a short-term chance on you for the other half, provided their credit check on you is favorable. If you don't have that much money, the Small Business Administration might go along

WORKSHEET

Self-employed

Net Income		$_____
Deduct Keogh Contribution	$_____	
Itemized Deductions	_____	
Exemptions (#____ x $750)	_____	
		=_____
Taxable Income		$_____
Federal Income Taxes		_____

- -

Spendable Income:

Net Income		$_____
Less Keogh Plan Contribution	$_____	
Less Itemized Deductions	_____	
Less Federal Income Taxes	_____	
Less Life & Health Premiums	_____	
Total		=_____
Spendable Income		$_____

WORKSHEET

Professional Corporation

Corporation Net Income		$_____
Deduct Your Salary	$_____	
Deduct Retirement Plan Contribution	_____	
Deduct Life & Health Insurance Premium	_____	
Total		=_____
Corporation Taxable Income		$_____

- -

Spendable Income:

Your Salary		$_____
Less Federal Income Taxes	$_____	
Less Itemized Deductions	_____	
Total		=_____
Spendable Income		$_____

with you and guarantee 90 percent of what you need. The bank would probably set a seven-year term for paying it back and charge one point higher than the prime lending rate.

Your capital investment needs could also be reduced through the leasing of equipment and/or financing it through the supplier.

Loans To and From The Corporation. This would be a good point to mention several ways in which corporations and their employees can benefit from lending each other money.

It is common practice among incorporators putting up the initial capital for a corporation to lend the corporation a portion of the capital rather than pay it all in for shares of stock. Subsequently from its earnings the corporation repays the loan or loans with some stated amount of interest. What would otherwise be classified as salary or dividends and therefore taxable income to the shareholders is merely repayment of a loan and therefore not taxable. The interest, of course, is taxable income for the shareholder and a deductible expense for the corporation. The IRS will hold still for only so much of this, though. To be quite safe you had better not furnish capital in a ratio of loans to stock purchases any greater than two to

one. More than that and IRS might call it a "thin" corporation, meaning thinly capitalized, and challenge its corporation status.

Later, when the corporation is really generating income, it can lend its employees money at favorable rates of interest for such worthwhile purposes as buying a home, marrying-off a daughter or educating a child.

Starting the Ball Rolling. Up to this point we have been discussing the advantages and problems of incorporation so that you can make a more educated decision about taking the step. You are probably still not totally sure that you should, or even more than half sure. You definitely have not canceled the thought, however, or you would have closed the book before this. In the next chapter we will discuss the actual steps to take in planning, forming, and operating a professional corporation. That should help you further along toward a decision — a decision that you might not make until some time after you have finished the book, have talked to friends and advisors, have picked up the book again and maybe other references too. Then finally you might do it — or continue to put off any decision. In any case, the next thing to do is to turn the page.

How to Form a
Professional Corporation
The Planning

We have already discussed most of a professional corporation's features, its advantages and disadvantages, things to look for and to look out for. Mostly, the discussion has been general, if not superficial, for three reasons:

(1) Too much detail destroys perspective. We have given you only the most important points in order to keep the scope within your vision.

(2) Thus, having gotten a grasp of the picture and at least in inclination toward forming a corporation, you could then zero in on the details.

(3) Because there are differences—black, white and gray—among the many government jurisdictions in our country and because our including copies of the actual laws or even abstracts of each would be superfluous, prohibitively expensive, and physically impractical, we have necessarily dealt in similarities and important differences. You will want to familiarize yourself with the professional and business corporation laws of the state in which you intend to incorporate. Depending on the state, it will take you anywhere from a few minutes to an hour or two to read what the law says.

There is a good deal of overlap between planning and implementing, but for the purpose of organizing the subject into more easily manageable chunks, let's divide the subject that way. We will discuss planning in this chapter and implementation in the next.

Get a Copy of Your State Law. In the appendix of this book, listed alphabetically by state, you will find the reference numbers for the law or laws governing professional corporations in that state. You will also find the address of the state office (usually the secretary of state) to which you should direct your request. Most of the states provide copies of the law and some or all the forms you will need for incorporation, but several do not. For those few, you will have to go to a law library and look up the reference given in the appendix (or ask your attorney to do so). Several of the states refer inquiries to a printer who handles the distribution for them; in such cases we have listed the printer. They, and several of the states who supply the literature directly, will bill you anywhere from one to twelve dollars or so. Most are free or about two dollars.

In most states two statutes cover everything—a professional corporation law for all professions and a general or business law covering the necessary points common to all corporations. Because several states have a separate law for each major profession, you should identify your profession when you write.

If you are not a lawyer, you might think that reading original law is a futile exercise. Even many lawyers hate to read legal language. Be assured, however, that what you will read is in clear language and can be understood easily enough by anyone who has graduated from college. It will be a small and worthwhile chore for helping to accomplish a very large and important project.

Choose a Name. We discussed this subject in the last chapter. Once you have obtained a copy of your state law and/or have consulted your professional regulating board, you will know what the requirements and limitations are. You should start thinking about it early, not because it might be difficult, but because you will want to "try it on" mentally for a period of time to see how a candidate name feels. The new name (if it is actually new) will also be needed for all documents, forms and official correspondence.

Financial Statement. If you will have one or several partners, you will have to all lay your cards on the table in order to achieve the agreement needed on a number of major points. Better to get it straightened out in the beginning than to find you have an irreconcilable difference later. An obvious early bridge to cross is finances. If you have had partners and are only planning to convert the partnership into a corporation, most of the spade work is already done; you already have a good idea of what each of you is collecting in fees and what your fiscal philosophies are. If you're going together for the first time, you will have to pool your information. Even if you have been practicing alone, you will have to take a hard look at your income and expenses with a thought about an incorporated future.

With partners you will have to discuss a fee structure for the corporation. You will have to agree on how to allocate income, capital, compensation and investments; and these will be a reflection of your collective interests regarding current income and fringe benefits versus investment for retirement. These discussions might also involve your accountant, banker and insurance man, since they will inevitably be involved anyway. (Just remember that while bankers and insurance salesmen do not charge for their time, accountants and lawyers usually do.) The basic idea is to see what you have to work with, what future expectations will be, and within those frameworks decide what you want to do. You can start from either direction: Establish your wishes for retirement and work backward to current needs and wants, then adjust; or figure your current needs and wants then see what the balance will do for you when finally converted to retirement income, and then make adjustments. Either way, you will early get into:

The Retirement Plan. Keep your Keogh? If not, what does one do with it? Rather than suffer the penalties that come from canceling it, just suspend it. You can always return to it and pick up where you left off if for some reason in the future you want to. Your decision will depend on how long you have had it, which in turn will determine how much is tied up and what the penalty will actually be in keeping it or dropping it for a qualified corporate plan.

What are the ages of the employees? How much can the corporation contribute? How big will the corporation be? What kind of turnover should be allowed for? What will be the retirement age? Will part-time service or consultation after retirement be perissible? These are many more questions will have to be answered before a plan can be written. This, the most complicated feature of an incorporation plan, will require the advice of experts on the subject. It will be their job, with your help, to determine the kind of plan (profit-sharing, money-purchase or fixed-benefit pension, etc.), the method of funding (percentage of profits, fixed sum, etc.), benefit formula (flat-payment, earnings, length-of-service, earnings-and-service, etc.), vesting rights, withdrawal and loan rights, forfeiture allocations, integration with Social Security, disability and beneficiary payments and many others.

The plan will have to be committed to writing in detail, presented to all the employees and submitted to the IRS. (You have to watch out for discrimination against non-professional help: If the plan arbitrarily favors the professionals, the IRS will disqualify it; if its benefits are not commensurate with investment and responsibility, it is not fair to the professionals.) Detailed books must be kept and annual reports submitted to IRS. It is certainly no part-time task for a preoccupied doctor, lawyer, engineer or anyone.

So who will provide the expert guidance and administration? Special departments of banks and trust companies provide such service. So do insurance underwriters, mutual fund management companies, investment houses and special investment counselors. Since an insurance carrier will understandably be slanted toward insurance-funded plans and a stock brokerage toward common stocks and mutual funds, a talk with several sources would be advisable.

One company that can provide virtually a total service in this connection is the Company Corporation Financial Services (CCFS). Its system involves a total financial planning service for its clients, including guidance in setting up corporate benefit plans such as pension, profit-sharing, and money-purchase plans and other tax-deductible programs. It designs all plans in accordance with your specific goals, both short- and long-range, and is coordinated with your accountant, attorney or other counsel of your choice. You can obtain complete information free of any obligation by writing the CCFS, Delaware Trust Plaza, 1800 Pennsylvania Avenue, Wilmington, Delaware 19806.

Your professional colleagues and business friends can cite their experiences, too; and even though they probably could not give you all the details of their own plans, they could render an opinion on its performance and steer you toward reliable assistance. Finally, you can supplement the personal expert help with reading on your own. In addition to the public and special libraries, the better book stores and mail-order business publication houses will have literature on pension plans. One good reference among many is listed in the bibliography of this book.*

Medical Reimbursement Plan. The Internal Revenue Code clearly states that payments made by an employer on behalf of its employees, including health insurance premiums, will not be taxed as income to the employee and will be deductible expenses for the employer. The allowable coverage extends to the employee's dependents as well.

Furthermore, and unlike the IRC restrictions on employee discrimination in pension plans, the medical and disability plans do not have to be offered to all employees, and an employer can provide different plans for different classes of employees. A note of caution, however: If a plan is available only to shareholder-employees, and particularly if only certain employees qualify to be shareholders as in the case of professional corporations, the IRS might say that the plan's beneficiaries are shareholders but not employees and that therefore the corporation cannot deduct the cost and the stockholders must report the payments as dividends. So if the plan, or plans, can include all employees, the IRS

---

* Institute for Business Planning, Inc., *PROFESSIONAL CORPORATION DESK BOOK.*

would have no case against the employee status of the shareholders. The extra cost would partially or totally nullify the corporate deductions benefit but would not be a net loss if this form of additional compensation to the nonprofessional employees were properly "merchandised" to them.*

The big decisions for the planners of the corporation involve the cost of maintaining employees' salaries while they are disabled. How much and how long can the corporation afford, even under an insurance-funded program? And what if two or more income-producers are disabled at the same time, what schedule of reduced compensation should apply, considering also that substitute help will be needed or income will be reduced, or both?

In extending benefits to employee dependents, death benefits should also be written so that maximum benefits for the beneficiaries can be obtained. The lump sum, income-tax-free payment of $5,000 and any other payments to beneficiaries should be set up in advance to be paid to an estate trustee rather than directly to the survivors, an important measure for avoiding estate taxes.

The following list of totally reimbursable and deductible items (except for payments otherwise reimbursed) is provided as emphasis on how broad this benefit of incorporation can be:

Ambulance service

Artificial limbs or teeth

Birth control pills and devices prescribed

Christian Science practitioner fees

Crutches and braces

Doctor (all types) and dental fees

Drugs and medicines

Eyeglasses, including contact lenses and their maintenance

Hearing aids and their upkeep

Hospital expenses

Laboratory fees

Nursing services (including board)

Prescribed items by physicians, including air conditioning and filtration, trips, health clubs, special equipment, special foods, therapy, vitamins and minerals, wheel chairs, X-rays, etc.

Psychiatric care

Transportation for medical care

Insurance. You will undoubtedly want to give each professional employee a minimum of $50,000 group term insurance, since that amount is tax-free to the employee. Beyond that, because of a low rate set by the IRS, group term insurance is taxable as income, but the additional coverage is a true bargain.

As for group ordinary life policies, you can plan to have the corporation pay the premiums for employees and deduct them also as a business cost. The employees pay tax on a portion of the premiums as income for this kind of coverage.

The corporation should also insure

---

* A sample medical reimbursement plan is contained in the appendix.

itself against property loss and liability of all the usual kinds, including malpractice.

Capitalization and Stock. Unlike a manufacturing or sales company, a service company — especially a professional service company — does not have to make a large investment in capital assets, such as plan, equipment, raw materials and inventory. In most cases you will need only office space, furnishings and some office and technical equipment. If these needs will merely be transferred from a partnership to the corporation in exchange for shares, cash needs will be small. You will need operating funds, of course, to cover your overhead, but this money will not enter into your plans for capitalizing the corporation. In some states you will have to put up a stipulated minimum, although the amount is usually no more than you would need anyway.

Now, how many shares? What kind of stock? Any reason for having other than common stock? In some states that is all you can have anyway. Par value? In only a couple of states is there a lower filing fee for a par value corporation, and simplicity, at least, indicates no-par stock for your corporation almost everywhere. Usually, a thousand shares suits most small corporations and this number results in minimum filing fees in most states. These are decisions you will have to make in advance, since the information must be stated in the articles of incorporation and on the stock certificates, which you might want to have printed* even if you can use a standard certificate and merely fill in the blanks.

Much more important than those decisions is the value to place in each share. Before you can divide a certain number of shares into a total corporation value and call that the value-per-share, you have to establish the total value and you have to decide how many shares to issue. The number of shares can be any number that is evenly divisible into the established total value, but keeping the number few can save you printing costs if nothing else. Your filing fee will depend on the amount of capitalization and/or the number of shares.

As for the total value, the obvious starting place is the physical assets plus any investments. Probably that should also be the stopping place, and here is why: Even though logic and pride assert that the practice, consisting of accounts-receivable, work-in-progress and goodwill, is worth far more than the mere physical and investment assets, if you base the value of each share on such true value of the practice, you can possibly run into trouble from several situations:

(1) At incorporation. Even though Section 351 of the Internal

---

* The Professional Corporation Co., 507 Beneficial Bldg., Wilmington, Delaware 19801, can furnish you with a corporate kit for any state. It includes 20 lithographed stock certificates, printed minutes and bylaws, a corporate seal and a vinyl-covered binder and slipcase for $35.00.

Revenue Code allows the tax-free transfer of assets to the new corporation, it does not protect the individuals involved from later getting taxed on their receivables generated before incorporation, if those accounts are included in the valuation of the corporation's shares. For this reason alone, if your corporation, like most professional corporations, uses cash-basis accounting, it would be better to keep the value-per-share low by not including accounts receivable, work-in-progress or goodwill in the value of a share. The problem is one called "collapsible corporation." The collapsible corporation status, an affliction devoutly to be avoided, is a status the IRS sometimes tries to pin on a corporation that is based on cash-basis accounting and personal service fees. To oversimplify for the sake of understanding the term, a collapsible corporation is one, according to the IRS, which has virtually nothing left to it if you dismiss its assets based on cash received for personal reputation and service. Without those, it "collapses." The IRS has taken the position that the technicality of incorporation does not change what is truly personal

income into corporate profits taxable as capital gains. Section 341 of the IRC was in fact enacted expressly to prevent the conversion of ordinary income to capital gains, thereby avoiding a higher tax rate on the income. But if the accounts-receivable, work-in-progress and goodwill never get mixed up in the value of the corporation's stock, there would be no basis for this kind of tax penalty in transactions involving the stock.

(2) Merger of a one-man practice or partnership into an already existing professional corporation. Section 351 allows tax-free transfer of assets only if immediately after the transfer the person(s) effecting the transfer can claim at least 80 percent ownership of all shares of the corporation. Since that would be highly unlikely in a merger, those assets transferred to the corporation could be taxed. Better to leave the receivables outside the corporation and collect them as an individual.

(3) The young professional who later might consider joining the corporation at your earnest invitation. He does not have to be a shareholder in order to

practice for the corporation, but you can understand his wanting to own shares. If he sees a prohibitive price tag on each share, he might correctly conclude that he could not for a long time, at best, wield any power or influence in the affairs of the corporation. You could, of course, issue him shares based somehow on an estimate of his own professional value to the corporation. But it would be an arbitrary reward, and perhaps not possible if enough voting strength resented giving a rank newcomer an asset that their long investment of time and energy, their experience and reputations earned. Furthermore, unless the shares were given from treasury stock (shares held by the corporation instead of having been issued or reissued), they would possibly be shares purchased at the same high price from a retiring, deceased or otherwise departed employee. Can the corporation pay out a large sum of money for shares they then turn over free to a new employee? Even if the redemption at retirement were funded by insurance, it would still be a cost to the corporation. Finally, the shares given to the new employee could very well

be called taxable income by IRS.

(4) The old professional who by law has to sell his shares when he stops practicing. A high price per share makes them difficult to sell to any other professional who would be welcomed by the other employees. Even selling them to the corporation, which is required by law if they are not sold to another person licensed by the state in the same profession, could be a tough proposition for the corporation. Since they would be purchased with after-tax dollars, the corporation's revenue-producers in, say, the 50 percent tax bracket would have to bring in twice the trade value of the shares in order to redeem them. Moreover, the retiree would have to pay capital gains on the sale if each share reflected an increased value in the assets of the corporation. Or worse, if IRS considers the corporation to be a collapsible corporation, he would be taxed on his profit at the ordinary income rate instead of the capital gains rate.

(5) Liquidation of the corporation. If the value of the shares is

based mainly on cash receivables, work-in-progress and goodwill, the IRS could conceivably tax the liquidated (distributed) assets as those of a collapsible corporation. Moreover, liquidations under Section 337 or 333 might not be possible. These sections of the IRC eliminate double taxation or defer gains at the liquidation of a corporation. To avoid such an unhappy development, the value of all accounts-receivable and work-in-progress should be liquidated — totally or as much as possible — by collecting and distributing the value before dissolving the corporation.

In summary, for the reasons listed above, it is to the advantage of all involved in the corporation to keep the value of shares relatively low by basing it on capital assets and the value of investments. In fact, it would be a good idea to emphasize the omission by drawing up an agreement for all principals to sign, stating that they place no value on receivables, work-in-progress or good will. The value will still be there should the corporation wish to borrow money or otherwise qualify itself, but the tax threat will be reduced.

Compensation. A one-man corporation has only to consider how to distribute his corporation's undistributed income among salary, dividends and accumulated capital. Nevertheless, that's a serious matter we will get to in a moment. The partners forming a corporation will also have to look at their individual fees going back over several years and consider any capital assets contributed to the corporation, what to do about periods of part-time service, leaves of absence (for professional purposes or personal), relative work loads and other matters in order to arrive at an equitable compensation structure for each of the income-producers.

Both the one-man corporation and the converted partnership will have to keep the IRS in mind when planning the compensation structure. One of the IRS attack-points on the legitimacy of a professional corporation is whether the corporation pays dividends and how much. Another issue is "reasonable salary." Their point has been that a corporation that merely collects fees and forwards them all to the respective principals is not a corporation but a pipeline.

One overriding purpose of a corporation is to make a profit, and if a corporation consistently shows no profit because all its income goes to overhead (salaries), it is not fulfilling its justification for existence. So the IRS might try to call it void and not allow its deductions for salaries, bonuses and investments. They would rather collect a tax on dividend income to the employee-shareholders than have that part of corporate income removed from taxable income by being paid out as salaries.

But, you say, they collect it from the individual, and the high end of a salary pays the highest percentage tax. Yes, but do not forget deferred salaries and bonuses that are ear-marked for payment after retirement and are not taxable during the current year. And don't overlook the 50 percent rule which protects an individual's *earned* income over the 50 percent tax bracket. A person earning as little as $38,000 taxable income can benefit from that measure. Even if the salaries are about the same as the individual incomes before incorporation, if that leaves nothing for the payment of dividends, Internal Revenue has called the salaries unreasonable.

In theory, the small corporation particularly finds itself in something of a quandary: If it pays large dividends (which gains nothing for a close corporation not trying to attract capital from outside investors), it gets hit with double taxation, and the dividends do not qualify for the 50 percent tax limit on earned income; if it distributes the income as salaries, IRS might call the salaries unreasonably high; and if the corporation lets the excess accumulate, IRS might call it a personal holding company and tax the accumulation at a confiscatory rate of 70 percent. We said earlier that a company is allowed a reasonable accumulation of income without being taxed on it — up to a maximum of $150,000 over its lifetime. But we were not talking about the

possibility now and then of a challenge by IRS on a small professional corporation as a personal holding company.

The risk of this has been nearly eliminated by IRS defeats in the tax courts, and today, yours would have to be a fairly blatant example among personal holding company types for the IRS to risk still another defeat. If they challenge anything, it would be more likely your salary as unreasonable, and if upheld by the claims court, call some arbitrary amount of your salary (and your fellow employees' salaries) dividends. This would especially be true if salaries were geared to corporate income as a percentage or if an increase in corporate income were distributed solely through salary increases or bonuses and if no or very low dividends were paid. Salaries should be paid on a regular schedule, and increases should be explained in the minutes as justified not by increased profit but by an increase in productivity, cost-of-living increase and such as that.

Most professional corporations, however, can go to tax court on the precedent set by the case of *Klamath Medical Services Bureau* (29 TC 339, 1957) and expect dismissal, if it ever came to surrender or fight. In that case, the court held that, where a business is a service business depending on the billings of professionals for its income, reasonable compensation for the professional means up to 100 percent of his billings, no part of which will be treated as dividends.

All matters considered with respect to low odds and favorable legal precedents, prudence would still suggest a conservative stance without imposing serious financial handicaps on the corporation or its shareholders. Essentially, this means to pay salaries that are as high as the going rate for the same service and quality of service in the same market, leave a little to accumulate, then pay the remainder as dividends, and at all times and places have the corporation responsible for assigning services performed by the employees. Incidentally, there could be some extra room in the corporation's fringe benefit program for a part of the surplus income. This would depend on the kinds of programs the corporation has and the formulas for funding them. Too much though, and IRS might also take a swing at them as excessive.

In addition to fringe benefits covered separately elsewhere, we should here discuss the compensation items of dividend and bonus payments, paid vacations and holidays, compensation for services performed outside of regular work hours, company-paid expenses and maintaining professional competency through special education.

On an accrual basis of accounting (credited when earned) as opposed to a cash basis (credited when paid), a bonus must be paid within two and a half months after the end of the corporation's fiscal or calendar year for the corporation to claim it as a deduction for that year. Bonuses, like dividends, are a part of the pie-dividing process at year's end and therefore should not be delayed if the corporation wants to deduct them in the year earned. The power to declare dividends, like bonuses, should be stated in the bylaws, with such details as who decides the amounts to be paid for each, the formula for allocating the bonus pool among employees, the method of payment (lump sum or installment, cash or stock), or even whether either dividends or bonuses can be paid at the end of a slow year.

You will undoubtedly decide to pattern your schedule of holidays and vacations after the prevailing practice in business generally and for your state specifically. Salaried employees in business usually are not relieved of any work during the time they are on vacation; it is still there waiting for them when they get back. But remember (as who in health service could forget!) in some professions arrangements have to be made to cover such "free" periods. For services that won't wait, other persons have to fill the gap. If outside help is enlisted it will have to be paid for, obviously, and the compensation structure of your corporation will have to allow for it. If coverage is handled internally, whether the extra burden is compensated by money or reciprocal service, a formula decided in advance and written into each employment contract can preclude misunderstandings and friction later on. Keep in mind, incidentally, that a statement of hiring outside help or assigning coverage internally during absences fortifies the corporation's position against a possible IRS personal holding company challenge.

If an employee is required by his employer to report business expenses paid on behalf of the employer, the employee does not have to report those expenses on his personal income tax. You can handle it either way — have employees claim business expenses or have the corporation claim them — but the method should be stated in writing in the compensation paragraph of the bylaws and in the employment contracts. A usual part of company expense is automotive transportation. Companies either pay employees the going per-mile rate for use of their private car on company business, or the company provides a car and charges the employees a per-mile rate for personal use. The corporation can own the car and other equipment, quarters and furnishings or can lease them — the choice bearing on a variety of considerations in each case.

Special courses and training to maintain your professional competency are deductible expenses for the corporation. So also are registration and initiation fees and dues to professional societies, clubs, seminars and conventions. Travel expenses to such events are likewise deductible, or at least a portion of them if you combine nonprofessional activities with the professional events.

The planning part, aside from choosing what kind and how much coverage you want, involves the cost of it all. Just remember that its being "free" to the employees and deductible from corporate income does not mean that a major part of its cost will not come out of corporate income, thereby affecting other compensation.

Transfer of Assets. At this important crossroads in your life, you might be tempted to throw out everything old and start with everything new in the new corporation — new furniture and furnishings, new automobile, new equipment sporting some convenience features your present equipment doesn't have. You will of necessity start off with some things new, such as files, books, forms and stationery. But better take a second look at the rest of it.

It is true that you will have to put a value on everything you contribute to the corporation and that selling the old stuff or turning it in for credit against new items will pin down the values more easily. Suppose, however, that everything you will transfer has been partially or fully depreciated? If the object in keeping it is to avoid or reduce taxes, you might as well get rid of it, since you can transfer anything you want without paying taxes on the liquidation of the old practice. Therefore, its value for tax purposes is unimportant. If your object, however, is to keep down investment costs, you would be wise to hold on to the old stuff for a while. First of all, you will never get in the marketplace or trade-in their respective replacement values. Secondly, if you are joining forces with another person or several, your high-value contribution might make difficult the equitable distribution of shares. And finally, after consolidation with the others, you might find that your new acquisitions do not fit the needs of the consolidated practice; and then you will really take a loss in converting the almost-new assets to something else.

We have already mentioned the tax-free transfer of assets under Section 351. IRS will recognize no gains or losses for tax purposes if immediately following incorporation at least 80 percent of the stock is owned by the persons transferring the properties. The latter stipulation is no problem for the owners of a new corporation. In the case of a merger, however, the smaller of two corporations or the newcomer individual(s) would be penalized in the transfer of assets having a high market value, since they would not hold 80 percent of the stock in the corporation immediately after the transfer of assets. Here, then, is another instance in which old assets should not be replaced just prior to incorporation.

The persons transferring the assets will have to report the action on their individual income tax returns for the year of transfer, giving a description of the property, its fair market value, the value of the stock for which it was traded and a statement that no money or property was received for the assets and no liabilities assumed by the corporation.

Any obligations, however, in the nature of loans outstanding, leases in force, or mortgages, should usually be assumed by the corporation.

Last but not least among important items to consider in the transfer of assets and liabilities is accounts payable. In a Section 351 transfer these should *not* be transferred to the corporation from a partnership operating on cash-basis accounting. If they are, they will not be deductible to the corporation when they are paid, and they will not be deductible against the personal income of the partners either. In short, they will be a total loss as a tax deduction. So plan to keep the old partnership in existence until all outstanding debts are paid. Then they will be deductible in the dissolution of the partnership.

How to Form a
Professional Corporation
Implementing the Plan

If your decision to incorporate has survived the planning stage, you are now ready to implement the plan. You can, of course, back out of the deal at any point, before incorporation or after, and not necessarily suffer any severe financial penalties. The time and energy you put into it, however, not to mention the cost of expert advice and service, if you decide to use it, will be a loss more or less great depending on how far into the matter you have progressed.

Assuming that the light is green after all the preliminary thought and planning, the next steps follow, not necessarily in the sequence given:

Agreement to Incorporate. Most incorporators skip this step as unnecessary. Since it is an agreement to do what you agree to do in the articles of incorporation and bylaws, but probably in less

detail, we feel it is superfluous. We mention it because the subject might arise or because you might want to tell your attorney in advance that you see no purpose in spending extra time and money on an agreement to an agreement.

Articles of Incorporation. This basic document is required in all states. State law invariably details the information required in the articles, and some states also require that you use an official form; others give you the option of using the form provided or your own. (The specimen tear-out form in the appendix is usable in most states or it can be used as a guide.) A state sometimes stipulates the size of paper, type and other specifications you must follow if you are preparing your own copy. Whatever the specific form, the information required in your articles of incorporation will be (not necessarily in this order):

— Name of Corporation. See earlier discussion on the choice of a name. A preliminary check for duplication and reservation of your choice could save you from a last-minute snag; if the name is available, for a small fee the state will hold it for you for three to six months, depending on the state. You can skip the preliminary check, however, and the secretary of state will notify you of any name problems after you have filed your articles.

— Purpose of the Corporation. In the case of a professional corporation, the purpose will be limited by law to the practice of the profession or of certain related professions. But the purpose should be stated as broadly within that limitation as possible so as not to restrict its future activities. The statement of purpose will also assert that the corporation will not engage in any business activity other than what is required to operate the corporation for professional service.

— Powers of the Corporation. The distinction between the purpose and the powers of a corporation is important. The powers clause spells out in some detail the rights and intentions of the corporation within the scope of its purpose and the limitations of

the law. A professional corporation, for example, will buy, own and sell property, invest in stocks, bonds and other securities, lend and borrow money, lease equipment and property and do anything else desirable and necessary for the performing of professional services.

— Principal Office Location. Almost always a professional corporation will be located in the same state in which it is incorporated. But it might have branch offices in the same state or in different states. Its principal office, even, might be in another state, depending on the states involved. The only requirement common to all states is that any member of a professional corporation practicing in the state must be licensed by the state to practice that profession. Many states, however, will not allow a corporation to practice outside the state, and some also will not allow alien professional corporations to practice within the state. Whatever the rule, the address of the principal office must be given in the articles of incorporation. As discussed previously, it usually pays to engage a registered agent who will act as your permanent official office for incorporation purposes.

— Registered Agent. States that

allow a foreign-based professional corporation to practice in the state will nevertheless require it to appoint an agent, who must be a natural resident of the state, or another corporation empowered to act as registered agent. Other states require an agent for serving of process on the corporation, if necessary. The agent might be a person or corporation located in the same county as the principal office of the professional corporation, or it might be the secretary of state, depending on the particular states that require an agent for this purpose. If your state is one that allows foreign-based professional corporations to practice in the state, you might choose to incorporate in one of the more attractive corporation states, such as Delaware. Without a legal Delaware residence, you would appoint an agent to represent you in that state. Retaining an agent need not be expensive. The Professional Corporation Company, for example, charges $50 a year. And for this fee you also get valuable information periodically which will keep you abreast of the latest tax rulings and legal avoidance of taxes as they pertain to corporations.

— Duration. With few exceptions, any corporation can have perpetual existence if it chooses. Most do so, since it places no requirement on the corporation to continue, at the same time that it precludes any future problems stemming from a terminal date. The intended life span of your corporation must usually be stated in the articles of incorporation. Otherwise, the state will automatically classify it as perpetual.

— Capitalization. The articles of incorporation will state the aggregate (total) number of shares the corporation will have authority to issue; the classes of stock and the number of shares for each class (probably all shares will be of the common stock class); what the par value of each share will be, including no par value; and whether they will all be voting shares or divided between voting and nonvoting in a number, ratio or some qualification explained in the clause. This article will also state the minimum amount of paid-in capital prerequisite to starting practice, an amount sometimes required by law, although the corporation is free to set a higher minimum. The incorporators' signatures at the end of the articles attest to having received the minimum in addition to swearing that all other information given is accurate and correct.

— Directors. The articles of incorporation should provide for a board of directors to run the affairs of the corporation. Depending on the number of shareholders, a professional corporation might have one, two, three, or more directors. Usually at least one director must be a shareholder, which means that he must be licensed in the state to practice the profession of the corporation. Otherwise, none of the directors would be permitted under law to handle policy matters involving professional decisions. Business and other nonprofessional matters would be the province of other than shareholder-directors. The directors usually elect the officers of the corporation, although the articles of incorporation could provide for election of officers as well as directors by the shareholders. The initial directors of the corporation will be listed by name and address. So also will be the incorporator(s).

Options to the Articles. In addition to the information given above, almost any other matters of pertinence may be included in the articles of incorporation. Or additional information or rules may be inserted instead in the bylaws. Or they can be entered in both. Examples of such items could include:

— Bylaws. The right or duty of the board of directors to adopt or amend bylaws may be stated in the articles of incorporation. Otherwise, the bylaws must be adopted or amended by the shareholders. Not all states require bylaws, but a professional corporation would be foolish to ignore them. Not only do they spell out the detailed rules of the corporation which if omitted could lead to disputes, oversights or errors, they also help confirm the corporate status in the face of tax collectors on the prowl for weak or infirm members of the herd.

— Preemptive Rights. This is the right of a shareholder to buy shares in proportion to the number of shares that he holds. It is a way of making a corporation go to its present shareholders first when issuing shares for additional capital. Preemptive rights are probably more important to a business corporation, since a professional corporation has a built-in check against outside financing, in the state laws limiting ownership to persons licensed to practice. Nevertheless, it could happen, and this tends to control ownership of the corporation. The right is assumed in some states if it is not specified in the articles of incorporation.

— Cumulative voting rights. This

feature allows a shareholder to vote all his shares for a single director. Normally a shareholder's total voting power can be cast for each of several directors in an election. With cumulative voting he can cast for a single candidate his total voting power times the number of directors to be elected, but he can then vote for no other candidate. This device makes it possible for a minority shareholder to elect a director of his choice. Without it his voice would be absent on certain matters when brought before the board. Cumulative voting might be included in the bylaws rather than in the articles of incorporation.

— Meetings. The articles of incorporation can provide for special meetings not covered in the bylaws and can also state the quorum requirements for shareholders' meetings, thereby possibly forestalling precipitous minority action on a quick-switch of quorum requirements.

Bylaws. (See sample in appendix.) The bylaws of a corporation are really its rule book. And the more detailed and comprehensive they are, the less will be left to chance or to decision-making at some inconvenient time later. Furthermore, the closer a professional corporation adheres to its bylaws, the better a chance it will have of convincing the IRS that it is a legitimate corporation and not a sham if the charge ever arises. State laws do not really require bylaws; most corporations have them for their own benefit. What will be contained in your own bylaws will be pretty much what you, the incorporators, want in them as long as they do not conflict with any item in quite detailed state corporation laws. Usually they include:

— Shareholder meetings. The annual meeting will be to elect directors for the coming year and to consider any other business brought before it at that time. The bylaws might provide that if the annual meeting fails to elect all the required directors (loses its quorum, for example), the directors will call a special meeting of the shareholders as soon as possible for that specific purpose. Other clauses include the calling of special shareholder meetings for any reason by minority shareholders, by the president or by the board of directors.

Notice of shareholder meetings should be explained: how the notice will be communicated, how soon before the meeting, who shall select the location (usually the directors); all relevant information should be written into the bylaws even if they are merely repetition of state law on the subject. Because of the closeness and informality of most professional corporations, the bylaws might declare legitimate any meeting called by a quorum of shareholders or directors without prior notice, to accommodate such situations as their finding themselves together and otherwise not able to hold a meeting because of the rule on notices.

Prior to the annual meeting, the corporation will prepare a voting list. This will show all the shareholders (of voting shares) and the number of shares owned by each. In a very small corporation obviously the information is well known. But remember the importance of doing everything that will enhance the formal aspect of the corporation.

The bylaws will state what constitutes a quorum at a shareholders' meeting. If this is not mentioned in the bylaws, state law usually says that a quorum will be a simple majority of issued shares.

Proxy voting in a professional corporation is allowed by some states and not by others, but no state allows a proxy vote to be given to a nonprofessional. Each stock certificate will carry that prohibition in writing, along with the prohibition against ownership by nonprofessionals. These points of law also should be reiterated in the bylaws.

Despite anyone's best attempts to cover everything in the bylaws so that special meetings will not have to be called repeatedly, problems will come up requiring official decisions. As these decisions are added to the bank of information in the bylaws, such special meetings will probably taper off. Meanwhile, some states have moved to streamline their laws to facilitate changes in a corporation's policy. Now action can be taken by common consent, through the mail or even by telephone. Most principals, in a small corporation especially, would be happy to sign a waiver of meeting and their consent to an action instead of getting involved in an unanticipated meeting. Unless this meeting by-pass is prohibited by law, it would be helpful to make it an option to the formal type of meeting.

— Directors. In a large corporation the authority for making day-to-day policy is sometimes vested in an executive committee, consisting of officers and directors. Whether this intermediary level is useful depends on the corporation, and in any situation the directors set the basic policy for the officers to follow in daily operations. Usually directors and officers are one and the same in a professional corporation, so the distinction in policy-making is rather academic. From another standpoint, however, the distinction better be made or problems with the IRS could ensue. If the officers make policy on-the-spot without bothering to add it as directors to the bylaws or, worse, make policy decisions that run contrary to the bylaws, IRS could logically charge that the articles of incorporation and bylaws are merely window-dressing and that the practice is not really a corporation. So once again, keep in mind that the greatest danger to the tax status, and therefore the effectiveness — indeed existence — of a professional corporation, particularly a small one, is laxity in adherence to the corporate form and function.

The bylaws should be specific about the number of directors, when they are to be elected by the shareholders (including any interim replacements), and what their terms will be. This would be an appropriate place in the bylaws to reiterate that a certain number (at least one in most states) of directors must be licensed to practice the profession in the state of incorporation. This would be the place also to provide for staggered terms, if desired, to preclude any abrupt alterations in basic policy result-ing from a complete change in directors at one time.

The schedule of directors' meetings, method of notification and allowable exceptions will be spelled out in the bylaws. Probably the directors will prefer not to set a rigid schedule because of conflicts with other affairs. The only problem to watch with a discretionary schedule is the tendency to put off the meetings. The IRS does not have a rule on the number and frequency of board meetings that constitute legitimacy, but the status of your corporation will be judged on this performance as much as on any other criteria. A suggestion is to require a meeting every month, or every other month, on a date to be determined within the required time limit. The bylaws should cover special meetings, too — who is authorized to call them, how it may be done and how much notice is required.

The bylaws will also give their definition of a quorum necessary for conducting a board meeting. Depending on what is decided, policy may be made actually by a minority of directors.

Directors' fees are usually omitted in a closely-held corporation, although travel expenses should be provided for. If a corporation has directors not actively involved in the practice, some kind of fee is often paid.

— Officers. Your bylaws will necessarily follow the state requirements regarding the qualifications of corporate officers. The requirements usually depend on how many shareholders a corporation has, the number determining how the usual four officer functions of president, vice-president, secretary and treasurer will be divided. Invariably, however, the president is a shareholder and can shoulder the duties of at least one other office — usually of the secretary. Other offices may, depending on the state, be filled by nonprofessional shareholders.

The compensation of officers will be set by the board of directors or by the single director if the corporation has only one. If the officers are also directors (and in professional corporations they usually are), an officer should be excused from the meeting during discussion of his compensation. In a small corporation such a practice might destroy the quorum or otherwise be totally impractical. The suggestion is just one more, where feasible to strengthen your position against the IRS.

The authority and duties of each office will be spelled out in the bylaws, generally along these lines:

(1) President — chief executive officer, directs the professional and business affairs of the corporation within the policy framework established by the board of directors. He is the final authority below the bylaws, directors and shareholders, usually attends and often presides over directors' and shareholders' meetings, is required to sign at least the most important documents of the corporation.

(2) Vice-President — is given the authority to act as president during the president's absence, at least over matters that cannot wait for the attention of the president.

(3) Treasurer — is responsible for the funds and securities of the corporation, must sign financial contracts and disbursements.

(4) Secretary — maintains the minutes of shareholders' and directors' meetings; sees that meeting schedules and notices are in line with the bylaws; keeps the shareholder register and stock transfer book; with the president validates stock certificates; custodian of corporate records and the corporate seal, fixes the seal to official documents, including stock certificates; and probably will perform other appropriate duties asked by the president or

the board.

— Banking. Even though it might be stated elsewhere, as for example in the duties of the treasurer, bank accounts and check-drawing authority should be dealt with in a separate section. This section will tell what the directors want in separation of funds for various purposes, the respective banks and names and numbers of the several accounts, even perhaps such details as the average balances to be carried in each.

The corporation will have to draw up a resolution to file with the bank or banks in addition to stating the intent in the bylaws. That will be the authority required by banks to do business with a corporation. In addition, the bank will probably want a resolution from the corporation for each loan, above a certain size anyway.

— Contracts. Besides loan contracts just mentioned, other substantial contracts will have to be authorized in the bylaws as a function of the board of directors, possibly with the authority delegated to one or more of the officers. Included will be leases on space and equipment, service and employment contracts and investment contracts.

— Fiscal Year. If a fiscal year is not selected and identified in the bylaws, the legal assumption is that the corporation is operating on a calendar year. The selection of a fiscal or calendar year is an important matter, since neglect in considering the pros and cons on taxes can mean a large opportunity missed or a large penalty incurred.

— Share Certificates. The bylaws should cite the restrictions and requirements for the transfer of shares and should also require those restrictions and requirements to be printed on each certificate. The principal restriction will be against the transfer to anyone who is not licensed to practice the profession in the state or states in which the corporation is authorized to provide the professional services. The main requirement will be the surrender, within a specified period of time stated in the law, of all shares by anyone whose license to practice has been discontinued.

— Dividends. Even though the authority to pay dividends is inherent in all corporations, this right should be written into the bylaws. The determination of whether to pay and how much to pay will be made by the board of directors. Whether the dividends are declared and paid on a periodical or annual basis could be specified in the bylaws.

— Indemnification. Officers and

directors should be indemnified for personal expenses incurred in actions against them while acting on behalf of the corporation. The clause will not provide legal protection against any officer or director charged with negligence, malfeasance, breach of duty, misconduct or any criminal charge, but otherwise should provide for reimbursement by the corporation.

Initial Minutes. The minutes of all directors' and shareholders' meetings will be kept in your corporation's minutes book and will be a record of all important matters involving the corporation. The minutes of the first, or organization, meeting of shareholders and of the board of directors will be drafted as documents preliminary to incorporation so that all items initially pertinent to the corporation will be reviewed and officially adopted. For the shareholders' meeting these will include but not be limited to:

— identification of the corporation by name and statutory address;
— a statement of the business reasons for incorporating the practice;
— announcement of initial directors' elections, with names and addresses of elected directors;
— adoption of the initial bylaws;
— resolution to authorize the directors to issue stock in a manner determined by them and the

bylaws;
— resolution to issue Section 1244 stock;
— resolution to file the certificate of incorporation and receipt of filing fees with the minutes.

For the initial board of directors' meeting, usually held immediately after the shareholders' meeting, the minutes should include:

— location and date of meeting;
— announcement of a quorum;
— election of a chairman and a secretary of the board;
— adoption of the official seal and the share and transfer book of the corporation;
— authorization of employment agreements for specific professionals;
— resolutions for delegation of specific duties, such as issuance of shares and making of contracts, to certain officers of the corporation;
— acceptance of the stock agreement and the banking agreement (separate resolutions), perhaps also the appointment of a corporate attorney, of the accountant and accounting-basis system;
— election of corporation officers, by title, name and address;
— resolution to accept any assets and liabilities of a specified partnership (or single private practice) in exchange for a certain number of shares in the corporation;

— resolution to reimburse the partnership or individuals for all expenses related to forming the corporation;

— adoption (in separate resolutions) of the predetermined retirement plan, medical payment plan and disability compensation plan.

Employment Agreement. To help protect the corporate status as well as to forestall disagreements, the corporation should have a contract with every licensed professional who will work for the corporation, whether he holds stock or doesn't. Included in the agreement should be:

— whether the employment for the corporation will be full-time or part-time;

— what the term of employment will be (until age 65?) unless terminated otherwise by either the employee or the corporation;

— compensation: the actual salary can be included or left out; if included, the agreement obviously will have to be updated periodically . . . the method of computing bonuses can be detailed or stated as a duty of the board of directors; the latter option is simpler and safer, vis-a-vis the IRS . . . at inception of the agreement or at a later date, it can also incorporate a deferred payment formula for reducing taxes on current income . . . and it can handle the payment of

compensation for professional service from outside sources, such as from royalties and honorariums;

— expenses: how out-of-pocket expenses are to be handled;

— duties: a vital part of the agreement, since it establishes that the corporation and not the employee determines service assignments, thereby helping to circumvent a personal holding company challenge;

— working hours, exceptions for covering other employees, etc.;

— working conditions: the facilities and personnel provided by the corporation;

— vacations and holidays: the holidays and vacation formula specified;

— leave-of-absence, for study, jury duty, military or other government service or personal reasons, should be dealt with in specifics;

— also, whether such ancillary activities as participation in professsional seminars should be fully compensated;

— who owns the employment records, the corporation or the employee;

— fringe benefits, even though these are covered separately in the respective plans, if only as acknowledgment that all are applicable to the employee;

— termination grounds and procedures, including compensation, transfer of shares, covenant not to compete for a specified period of time (of dubious legal value, but perhaps morally effective), ownership of facilities, and so forth.

Stock Agreement.* These are important to any corporation; for a professional corporation they are even more important because of the strict limitation placed on stock ownership by the law and by the various professional regulating boards. The professional corporation has the same interest in continuity and compatibility of ownership as any kind of corporation, so it will want qualified control over the ownership of its stock. Furthermore, its very existence might be jeopardized by a former employee who refused to surrender his ownership of shares despite the law. The law places the burden of owners' qualification on the corporation, and its position could be made more difficult without a signed agreement on this point. The agreement would also be useful in getting transfer of stock ownership from a deceased owner's estate; in providing for a fair redemption by the corporation on the retirement or death of each employee; in providing for ownership by new employees, perhaps on an installment basis (but not as compensation for services, which would make it taxable income).

The valuation of each share is another feature of paramount impor-

tance. Whether the value will include accounts-receivable, work-in-progress and good will, is a matter of choice. We would only remind you of the personal holding company problem that such valuation entails for a corporation using cash-basis accounting. With or without those items in the valuation, each share will be based on the value of the corporation's capital assets and investment equities. The values of these will have to be adjusted at least once a year in order to reflect current market indexes. If a given group of shares has to be valuated at some irregular point for redemption, the value would be based on the book value — perhaps adjusted to market value — at the end of the preceding business month. Because the funding of death and disability benefits is often done with insurance, any effect of an employee's termination on corporate insurance premiums and equity would also have to be weighed in the valuation. Moreover, the disposition of corporate policies on the employee would have to be written into the stock agreement.

The reason the stock agreement is so comprehensive is its function as a basic instrument of understanding between a corporation and its owners. Correlative to that fact is the following checklist of features that go into a sound agreement;
— identification of shareholder and the number of shares held;
— buy-sell restrictions: ownership limited to licensed, practicing

---

* Different terms are used by different persons, but the usual terms are "stock purchase agreement," "buy-sell agreement" or "stock restriction agreement."

members of the profession; and to prevent transfer to strangers, the other owners or the corporation get first option to redeem available shares;

— death or retirement arrangements for compensation and transfer;

— voluntary surrender otherwise, with compensation and transfer agreement;

— dismissal for cause, the causes detailed, which besides criminal or ethical culpability, might include simple incompatibility with a majority of the other shareholders;

— valuation of shares, as discussed above;

— amendments to the agreement must be in writing and signed by all parties, or by a majority of owners with the alternative of agreement or surrender of shares by dissenting minorities;

— disagreements can always arise, even with a well-drafted agreement, and provision should be made for submitting disputes to an arbitrator, which might be the professional licensing board or professional society, or the American Arbitration Association;

— a statement that the agreement is subject to the state laws governing such agreements;

— dissolution of the corporation, if for any reason it becomes necessary or desirable. The procedure to be followed would be written into the agreement.

In addition to the major items listed above and in the preceding chapter, the following details, requiring less planning but not less attention, must be accounted for during implementation of your corporation:

Certificate of License. Your state of incorporation might be one that requires the filing of a certificate of license as evidence that employee-shareholders are qualified and authorized to practice the profession in that state. The certification invariably comes from the regulating or licensing board for the profession. Your copy of the state law for professional corporations will say whether this step is mandatory.

Application for Federal Employer Identification Number. Your application to your local IRS branch on Form SS-4 should be made early, inasmuch as government bureaus sometimes move very slowly, and your paperwork would be handicapped without the number. It has to accompany all reports, such as income tax withholding and pension plans, submitted to Washington. Your state might also require an employer identification number, and you would be well advised to apply for it early for the same reason.

Filing W-4 Forms. Each employee, professional and nonprofessional, will have to file with the corporation a W-4 form, available from IRS, containing the employee's name, Social Security number and number of dependents (for withholding purposes). Later, the corporation will have to issue W-2 forms to employees for the filing of income tax reports. This would be an entirely new experience for a person who has been self-employed all his working career, and he might not know that the number of claimed exemptions may be arbitrarily increased or decreased to balance withholding with anticipated tax owed. (The increasing of exemptions, however, has to be based on a formula tied to previous tax refunds.)

Other Forms. We said earlier that one of the disadvantages of incorporating was the increase in paperwork, an increase small or burdensome depending on how large the corporation is, how large your unincorporated establishment was, and what kind of office help you have. Some, but unfortunately not all, the forms your corporation will (might not) have to file with the appropriate authorities include: Federal and state unemployment compensation, corporate income tax, franchise tax, tangible and intangible property tax, sales tax, real estate tax, narcotics licenses, registration of shares with the Division of Securities.

Stationery, Business Forms. You will need new stationery, even if the corporation retains the old partnership name, simply because the law usually requires

the professional corporation status to be indicated in one of several allowable ways. Besides, it is in your own interest to show wherever possible that it is a corporation. In addition to letterheads, memo and prescription pads, rubber stamps, envelopes, invoices and statements, labels and business cards, the name should be changed on any equipment carrying the old name, and new signs should be made for the yard, building, office door and so forth.

Listings. The city directory, telephone directory, business and professional references, and the post office will have to be notified of the name change, even if the address and telephone number(s) remain the same.

Vendors. All suppliers should be notified that as of a certain date the business will function under its new name and that all invoices and other communications should be addressed to the corporation as of that date. This includes utilities and subscriptions as well as service and materials vendors.

Announcements. You might have to ask your professional register how far you can go in announcing the inception of your corporation without having it classified as unethical advertising. If there is a distinct name change, particularly, you will have to notify your clients or patients and you will want to explain to them (in terms favorable to them as much as possible) why the change was made. You should also inform your professional societies, fraternities and professional publications, which will undoubtedly run an announcement for the benefit of you and your colleagues.

Contracts and Agreements. Contracts of whatever description — employee, bank loan, leases, service, construction, investment, insurance, etc. — will have to be changed to name the corporation as contractor for any contracts made before the incorporation, and which you want the corporation to assume. This item goes back to the early planning stage of the incorporation, because of its serious tax manifestations, and we only mention it here as a detail reminder. Agreements such as physicians have with hospitals and Blue Cross will also have to be changed.

Employees. Undoubtedly your regular employees will know about the incorporation well before it happens, but you would be wise to notify them in writing in advance of the date in any case. For employees working without a contract, the notice would be simply a courtesy and a precaution against later misunderstandings; but for employees working under contract with the single practice or partnership, it will be a legal necessity to tell the employees as well as to change the name on the contract.

Opening New Books. You definitely should not continue keeping records in the same ledgers, files and indexes as used in the previous operation. They should be filed away and a whole new set of books should be set up for the corporation. Anyway, the corporation will require records that you did not need before, such as separate accounts for officers' salaries, bonuses, dividends and expenses, for paid-in surplus, for medical, disability and life insurance plans, and for the retirement plan.

* * *

In conjunction with the events, projects and items discussed above (before some of them, following most of them), you will go through the motions of actually becoming incorporated. That part of it is almost the simplest of all — simpler in some states than in others, but surprisingly easy in any of them. In fact, just to illustrate the point we will pretend that one day you decide on impulse to change to a corporation. We will further assume that the state in which you decide to form your professional corporation is one of those with the simplest procedure. So you take the appropriate articles of incorporation form from the appendix of this book, fill it out and have it photocopied, have your signature(s) witnessed and notarized on both forms, attach a check to cover the necessary filing fees (less than a hundred dollars — much less in many states) and mail them to your registered agent if you are using one, or to the address for your state listed in the appendix. After the state office (usually the secretary of state) has found that your choice of name does not conflict with any other already authorized, the state officer certifies the original, compares the copy and certifies that it is a true copy, sends it to the county clerk for filing, returns the original to your registered agent or to you with a receipt for fees paid and your certificate of incorporation, and your corporation is in business as of the time and date entered on the certificate. The entire procedure has taken a few days to a few weeks.

In other states, you will have to obtain certification of your professional qualification from your professional regulating board before the secretary of state will certify your articles of incorporation. In others, the corporation does not start business officially until a copy of the certificate and articles of incorporation have been stamped and filed with the county clerk. Georgia and one or two other states require a corporation to post notice in a newspaper of general circulation in the county before the corporation becomes official. In Georgia, in fact, you must advertise your intention to incorporate each week for four weeks. There, also, a judge of the county superior court must review the articles of incorporation and the certificate from the secretary of state, then pass an order declaring the incorporation granted. Even then, the corporation is now allowed to start in business until an affidavit from the newspaper has been presented with the other documents to

the clerk of the county court, the clerk's fee has been paid and the documents stamped and filed. We single out Georgia, one of the more complicated states in which to incorporate, only to make a point: that the mechanics of incorporation, at worst, are not one of the more involved steps in the planning and incorporation of a business or a profession.

Indeed, for many professionals considering incorporation, we have dwelled too long on matters of no consequence, just as for others we have touched too lightly or not at all on matters of importance to them. As we said in the beginning, we would try to stay in the middle ground of greatest benefit to most professionals. The corporation that needs more than we have included can obviously get the help from its advisors or from one of the heavy, detailed tomes we feel discourage the average professional in need of help. We ourselves would not want to be guilty of discouraging anyone who could benefit from incorporating the practice. That is why at this point we emphasize our reason for including points that need not involve every reader — especially the reader who would be incorporating a one-man practice or a several-man partnership. You in that category, however, cannot take too seriously the matter of sticking to the corporate form and function like a leech. Yet if you do so, neither should you feel especially concerned about notices from the IRS. No one who itemizes deductions is immune from that unpleasantness, and it would be utter folly to penalize oneself in hard-earned cash just to reduce the odds of a tax investigation. If you are earnest and sincere, honest and businesslike, you should not get hurt. The IRS, as bad a reputation as it has, is really looking for two things: mistakes and criminal intent. Everyone makes mistakes, and they will treat you gently if you make one (although the mistake itself could really hurt). But if they catch you hiding income illegally, they might hit you with a vengeance.

Familiarize yourself with the law, get good counsel, heed the suggestions of this book, and generally keep alert to the business side of your practice. Then you will have just one more point to consider on your master checklist: Enjoy the tangible benefits and the great peace-of-mind that a corporation makes available to you.

Forming Your
Professional Corporation

When you form your professional corporation, you have three options from which to choose. They are:

* *Hire a lawyer* for the incorporation of your practice or profession
* *File your own corporate papers*
* *Engage the Professional Corporation Co.*

Hiring a Lawyer. When you hire a lawyer, he will arrange to obtain a registered agent and draw up your incorporation papers. Estimated costs of accomplishing this, *not including* your state's filing fees, are from $500 to $3,000 or more, for legal fees alone.

File your own papers. If you wish to file your own corporation papers using the specimen included in this book as a guide, you may do so without a lawyer.

You can act as your own registered agent, or hire one. Earlier in this book, there was a description of what services a registered agent provides. You can obtain all the necessary corporation documents and materials at a legal stationery store. Your initial cost would then be the state filing fees and registered agent fee. However, nearly all registered agents interviewed require forms to be submitted through a lawyer. If this is the case, you must then hire a lawyer, and pay his or her fees.

Engage the Professional Corporation Co. The Professional Corporation Co. was established to provide the services needed nationwide by professionals. This can be accomplished at the lowest possible cost, with a minimum amount of time and effort on your part. It is the business of the Professional Corporation Co.

to provide these services throughout the country, and the procedures are streamlined to give the quickest and most complete service available.

The Professional Corporation Co.'s sole purpose is to work with professionals from all fields, including lawyers and accountants (and their clients), for the specific purpose of assisting them in filing their corporate papers and acting as their Registered Agent. As an individual, you (or your lawyer, accountant or other advisor) can complete the appropriate forms which are included in this book. Initial cost and fees for the service are $190.00. This fee includes the Registered Agent Fee for the first calendar year. A Corporate Kit is also included which contains a Corporate Seal, printed Stock Certificates and Bylaws. The annual fee thereafter payable to the Professional Corporation Co. is $50.00, which will provide you with a registered office in the state in which you practice.

Thus, by retaining the Professional Corporation Co., you can incorporate for a cost of $190.00. Your annual fees could be as low as $50.00 thereafter.* Your only other initial incorporate fees would be state filing fees** and/or any fees you may incur in talking with an accountant and/or lawyer.

For a complete description of all the services offered by the Professional Corporation Co., see the next page.

---

* All fees subject to change without prior notice.
** See section on State Filing Fees.

THE PROFESSIONAL CORPORATION CO.
SERVICES ARE DESCRIBED AS FOLLOWS

Initial Service:
1. Reservation of corporate name.
2. Provision of Registered Agent services in any state.
3. Filing of all documents with state corporation departments and other state agencies.
4. Supplying usable forms for incorporation in any state.
5. Preparation of checks for payments of initial recording fees.
6. Supplying corporate kit. This includes printed Stock Certificates, Corporate Seal and forms for minutes and bylaws.
7. Assistance with qualifying the corporation "to do business" in any state.

Continuing Service:
8. Act as Registered Agent in the state where you do business.
9. Forwarding of all legal documents such as annual reports from any Secretary of State.
10. Referral services to lawyers, accountants or other professionals.
11. Receipt and handling of service of process, and any legal documents served on the corporation promptly forwarded.
12. Supplying of printed information at least four times a year with tips on tax planning, corporate planning and other pertinent corporate matters.
13. Assistance in changes in the corporation's structure, such as: a name change, new class of stock, increase in number of shares, amending certificates, etc. Fees are billed as service is rendered.

If you choose to appoint the Professional Corporation Co. as your Registered Agent, what do you do next?
1. Choose a name.
*2. Decide on the number and value of shares (i.e., 1,000 shares at no par value).
*3. Choose Officers and Directors.
4. Complete the forms contained in the next few pages following State Filing Fee schedules. Be sure to sign and complete the Confidential Information Form as well as the Certificate of Incorporation (use the specimen as a convenient guide). This will take just a few moments. Sample Certificates of Incorporation herein included are accepted by most states. If a different form is required due to changes or requirements of state law, the Professional Corporation Co. will provide you with the correct form at no additional charge.
5. Tear out and mail forms with your payment of $190.00. Depending on the mails, you will receive an acknowledgement regarding the status of your corporation within two to three weeks.

These items are fully explained earlier in this book. As you can see, incorporation using the Professional Corporation Co. is extremely uncomplicated and quick. This remarkably easy system has been developed over many years in conjunction with The Company Corporation, which is the fastest growing Registered Agent in the United States, and serves many thousands of business corporations.

The following page provides a worksheet whereby you may make decisions regarding the particulars of your professional corporation.

WORKSHEET

1. Choose a name.

    First Choice _____

    Second Choice _____

    Alternative _____

2. Decide on number and value of shares.

    Number of Shares_____ Par Value_____ No Par Value_____

3. Choose Officers and Directors.

    Officers — First _____

                 Second _____

                  Alternative _____

    Directors — First _____

                  Second _____

                  Alternative _____

4. Complete the Certificate of Incorporation.

5. Mail to the Professional Corporation Co.

Determination of fee* payable to the Professional Corporation Co.

1.	First year Registered Agent Fee	$ 50.00
2.	Processing Incorporation Documents	85.00
3.	Reservation of Corporate Name	10.00
4.	Recording Document	10.00
	Sub Total	$155.00
5.	Deluxe Corporate Kit (vinyl coated with slip case; includes 20 lithographed Stock Certificates, Corporate Seal, Minutes and Bylaws)	35.00
	TOTAL	$190.00
	(Optional luxurious leatherbound corporate kit)	80.00
	OPTIONAL TOTAL	$235.00

Your only additional cost is for State Filing Fees which depend on the state in which you incorporate. State Filing Fees for professional corporations tend to follow the same guidelines and costs as do regular business corporations. However, there are a few exceptions to this and, of course, there are changes in them periodically.

A list of initial corporate filing costs for professional corporations begins on page 85.

In order to determine the approximate cost of filing a corporation in your state, review the list of states and find the one in which you are licensed and in which to incorporate. You can call or write the appropriate state agency to confirm the current exact figure if you wish. (To the best of our knowledge, the figures used in the next section are correct as of this writing.)

* All fees subject to change without prior notice.

TO BE SUBMITTED IN DUPLICATE

CONFIDENTIAL INFORMATION FORM

1. Name of Professional Corporation _____
   _____
   Alternate Name if above name is not available _____
   _____

2. Description of activities of corporation_____
   _____
   _____

3. Number of shares to be authorized by corporation without par value _____ with par value
   _____

4. Registered Agent service required in the following state or states:
   _____

5. Name and address of Officers of Corporation
   President _____ Address _____
   Vice President _____ Address _____
   Secretary _____ Address _____
   Treasurer _____ Address _____

5a. Name and Addresses of Directors of Corporation
   _____   _____
   _____   _____
   _____   _____

6. Name and Addresses of Incorporators (up to 3 in some states)
   _____   _____
   _____   _____
   _____   _____

7. Name and Address of Individual to whom correspondence regarding this corporation is to be directed
   _____Telephone Number_____

8. Any special instructions_____
   _____
   Where did you purchase this book? From an advertisement in_____
   Bookstore_____ Referred by _____ Other_____

9. Enclosed is payment in the amount of $_____ (total of your check should include state filing fee added to either $190 or $235 if leatherbound kit). (For faster service use certified check, treasurer's check or money order.)

10. Please accept my application for filing the enclosed corporation documents. I authorize you to proceed to reserve the above corporate name and to forward appropriate documentation and bill or credit me for any differences in filing fee. I certify that no personal legal advice or counsel has been given me by Professional Corporation Co.

_____
Signature of Applicant

Detach and mail this form to Professional Corporation Co., 507 Beneficial Bldg., Wilmington, Delaware 19801.

* All fees subject to change without notice.

TO BE SUBMITTED IN DUPLICATE

CONFIDENTIAL INFORMATION FORM

1. Name of Professional Corporation _____

   Alternate Name if above name is not available _____

2. Description of activities of corporation_____

3. Number of shares to be authorized by corporation without par value _____ with par value

   _____

4. Registered Agent service required in the following state or states:

   _____

5. Name and address of Officers of Corporation
   President _____ Address _____
   Vice President _____ Address _____
   Secretary _____ Address _____
   Treasurer _____ Address _____

5a. Name and Addresses of Directors of Corporation

   _____   _____
   _____   _____
   _____   _____

6. Name and Addresses of Incorporators (up to 3 in some states)

   _____   _____
   _____   _____
   _____   _____

7. Name and Address of Individual to whom correspondence regarding this corporation is to be directed

   _____
   _____Telephone Number_____

8. Any special instructions_____

   Where did you purchase this book? From an advertisement in_____
   Bookstore_____ Referred by_____ Other_____

9. Enclosed is payment in the amount of $_____ (total of your check should include state filing fee added to either $190 or $235 if leatherbound kit). (For faster service use certified check, treasurer's check or money order.)

10. Please accept my application for filing the enclosed corporation documents. I authorize you to proceed to reserve the above corporate name and to forward appropriate documentation and bill or credit me for any differences in filing fee. I certify that no personal legal advice or counsel has been given me by Professional Corporation Co.

   _____
   Signature of Applicant

Detach and mail this form to Professional Corporation Co., 507 Beneficial Bldg., Wilmington, Delaware 19801.

* All fees subject to change without notice.

ARTICLES OF INCORPORATION
OF
Jonas J. Jones, P. C.
(name of corporation)

The undersigned natural person(s), of the age of _21_ or more, acting to form a professional corporation under Chapter ____ *55B* ____ of the laws of *North Carolina* ____,
(statute(s) covering prof. corps.)   (state)
do hereby state the following:

ARTICLE I. The name of the corporation shall be *Jonas J. Jones P.C.* ____.

ARTICLE II. The address of the initial registered office of the corporation is *(leave address blank if using Professional Corporation Co. as Registered Agent)* and the name of the initial registered agent at such address is *(leave blank if using Professional Corporation Co.)*

ARTICLE III. The purpose for which the corporation is organized shall be to practice the profession of *medicine* : and to invest its funds in real estate, mortgages, stocks, bonds, or any other type of investment, or to own real or personal property necessary for the practice of that profession; and to perform such acts and conduct such business as may be permitted by the statutes governing professional corporations in this state.

ARTICLE IV. The total number of shares of stock which the corporation is authorized to have outstanding is *1,000*, defined as follows:

Class	No. Shares	Par Value
Common	*1,000*	*No Par*

The amount of stated capital with which the corporation shall begin business is $ *1,000.00* .

ARTICLE V. The names and addresses of the persons who are to act as incorporators are as follows:

Name	Address
Jonas J. Jones, M.D.	*74 Westview Dr., Durham, N.C.*
Marion M. White, M.D.	*32 Spring St. Durham, N.C.*
Sheila K. Doe, M.D.	*3011 Garden Blvd., Durham, N.C.*

ARTICLE VI. The number of directors constituting the initial board of directors is *three* ____, and the names and addresses of the persons who will serve as directors until the first annual meeting of shareholders or until their successors are elected are:

Name	Address
Jonas J Jones, M.D.	*74 Westview dr., Durham, N.C.*
Marion M. White, M.D.	*32 Spring St., Durham, N.C.*
Sheila K. Doe, M.D.	*3011 Garden Blvd, Durham, N.C.*

ARTICLE VII. All shareholders of the corporation shall be duly licensed to practice *Medicine* under the laws of *North Carolina* ____, and the original shareholders of the corporation are:

Name	Address
Jonas J. Jones, M.D.	*74 Westview Dr., Durham, N.C.*
Marion M. White, M.D.	*32 Spring St. Durham, N.C.*
Sheila K. Doe, M.D.	*3011 Garden Blvd, Durham, N.C.*

ARTICLE VIII. The following provisions are hereby adopted for the purpose of defining and regulating the authority of the corporation and of its stockholders, directors, and officers:

1. The original bylaws of the Corporation shall be the bylaws proposed and passed at the initial meeting of the incorporators and adopted by the board of directors. Additional by-laws and amendments to the current bylaws shall be voted upon at the annual meeting of stockholders; interim bylaws and amendments may be enacted by the board of directors, subject to ratification by the stockholders at the next annual meeting, but shall be in force until such ratification or rejection.

2. Any shareholder who for any reason shall have Corporation stock to sell shall offer these shares to all other shareholders and to the Corporation, at a price determined by the Stock-holder Agreement, and shall accept any offer of purchase under such Agreement before offering the stock to persons outside the Corporation.

3. Unscheduled meetings of the Directors may be called without advance notice by any Direc-tor or Officer of the Corporation, provided that a quorum of Directors agrees to the meeting and signifies waiver of notice by attendance at the meeting.

4. Business of the Corporation may be conducted without calling a meeting, provided that the action is submitted in writing to a quorum of Directors, whose signature to the action shall constitute a waiver of meeting and the same approval as a vote cast in person at a regular meeting.

5. The Corporation alone shall hold the power to assign the duties and service of its employ-ees, both regular and temporary, including employees substituting in an emergency or other unforeseen contingency.

ARTICLE IX. The duration of the corporation shall be ninety-nine (99) years.

We (I), the undersigned, being all the incorporators of the professional corporation identified above, declare that we have examined the foregoing this _____third_____ day of _____April_____, 19_77_, and do declare it to be true and correct.

	Name	Address
(Signed)	*Jonas J. Jones, M.D.* Jonas J. Jones, M.D.	74 Westview Dr. Durham, North Carolina
(Signed)	*Marion M. White, M.D.* Marion M. White, M.D.	32 Spring St. Durham, North Carolina
(Signed)	*Sheila K. Doe, M.D.* Sheila K. Doe, M.D.	3011 Garden Blvd. Durham, North Carolina

State of _North Carolina_   County of _Durham_

THIS IS TO CERTIFY that on this date _April 3, 1977_ before me, a notary public, personally appeared _Jonas J. Jones_, _Marion M. White_ and _Sheila K. Doe_ who I am satisfied are the persons named as incorporators and executors of the foregoing Articles of Incorporation, and who by their respective signatures in my presence have acknowledged the same as their voluntary act.

IN TESTIMONY WHEREOF, I have hereunto set my hand and affixed my official seal on the date given above.

H. L. Fordham (H. L. Fordham)
Notary Public

My commission expires: _Dec. 31, 1977_

ARTICLES OF INCORPORATION
OF

_____
(name of corporation)

The undersigned natural person(s), of the age of _____ or more, acting to form a professional corporation under Chapter _____ of the laws of _____,
(statute(s) covering prof. corps.)   (state)
do hereby state the following:

ARTICLE I. The name of the corporation shall be _____.

ARTICLE II. The address of the initial registered office of the corporation is_____
_____

and the name of the initial registered agent at such address is _____
_____

ARTICLE III. The purpose for which the corporation is organized shall be to practice the profession of _____ : and to invest its funds in real estate, mortgages, stocks, bonds, or any other type of investment, or to own real or personal property necessary for the practice of that profession; and to perform such acts and conduct such business as may be permitted by the statutes governing professional corporations in this state.

ARTICLE IV. The total number of shares of stock which the corporation is authorized to have outstanding is _____, defined as follows:

Class	No. Shares	Par Value

The amount of stated capital with which the corporation shall begin business is $_____ .

ARTICLE V. The names and addresses of the persons who are to act as incorporators are as follows:

Name	Address

ARTICLE VI. The number of directors constituting the initial board of directors is _____, and the names and addresses of the persons who will serve as directors until the first annual meeting of shareholders or until their successors are elected are:

Name	Address

ARTICLE VII. All shareholders of the corporation shall be duly licensed to practice _____ under the laws of _____, and the original shareholders of the corporation are:

Name	Address

ARTICLE VIII. The following provisions are hereby adopted for the purpose of defining and regulating the authority of the corporation and of its stockholders, directors, and officers:

1. The original bylaws of the Corporation shall be the bylaws proposed and passed at the initial meeting of the incorporators and adopted by the board of directors. Additional bylaws and amendments to the current bylaws shall be voted upon at the annual meeting of stockholders; interim bylaws and amendments may be enacted by the board of directors, subject to ratification by the stockholders at the next annual meeting, but shall be in force until such ratification or rejection.

2. Any shareholder who for any reason shall have Corporation stock to sell shall offer these shares to all other shareholders and to the Corporation, at a price determined by the Stockholder Agreement, and shall accept any offer of purchase under such Agreement before offering the stock to persons outside the Corporation.

3. Unscheduled meetings of the Directors may be called without advance notice by any Director or Officer of the Corporation, provided that a quorum of Directors agrees to the meeting and signifies waiver of notice by attendance at the meeting.

4. Business of the Corporation may be conducted without calling a meeting, provided that the action is submitted in writing to a quorum of Directors, whose signature to the action shall constitute a waiver of meeting and the same approval as a vote cast in person at a regular meeting.

5. The Corporation alone shall hold the power to assign the duties and service of its employees, both regular and temporary, including employees substituting in an emergency or other unforeseen contingency.

ARTICLE IX. The duration of the corporation shall be ninety-nine (99) years.

We (I), the undersigned, being all the incorporators of the professional corporation identified above, declare that we have examined the foregoing this _____ day of _____ , 19____ , and do declare it to be true and correct.

	Name	Address
(Signed)	_____	_____
	_____	_____
(Signed)	_____	_____
	_____	_____
(Signed)	_____	_____
	_____	_____

State of _____ , County of _____

THIS IS TO CERTIFY that on this date _____ before me, a notary public, personally appeared _____ , _____ and _____ who I am satisfied are the persons named as incorporators and executors of the foregoing Articles of Incorporation, and who by their respective signatures in my presence have acknowledged the same as their voluntary act.

IN TESTIMONY WHEREOF, I have hereunto set my hand and affixed my official seal on the date given above.

_____
Notary Public

My commission expires:

ARTICLES OF INCORPORATION
OF

_____

The undersigned natural person(s), of the age of _____ or more, acting to form **a** professional corporation under Chapter _____ of the laws of _____,
(statute(s) covering prof. corps.)   (state)
do hereby state the following:

ARTICLE I. The name of the corporation shall be _____.

ARTICLE II. The address of the initial registered office of the corporation is _____
_____

and the name of the initial registered agent at such address is _____
_____

ARTICLE III. The purpose for which the corporation is organized shall be to practice the profession **of**
_____ : and to invest its funds in real estate, mortgages, stocks, bonds, or any other type of investment, or to own real or personal property necessary for the practice of that profession; and to perform such acts and conduct such business as may be permitted by the statutes governing professional corporations in this state.

ARTICLE IV. The total number of shares of stock which the corporation is authorized to have outstanding is _____, defined as follows:

Class	No. Shares	Par Value

The amount of stated capital with which the corporation shall begin business is $_____ .

ARTICLE V. The names and addresses of the persons who are to act as incorporators are as follows:

Name	Address

ARTICLE VI. The number of directors constituting the initial board of directors is _____, and **the** names and addresses of the persons who will serve as directors until the first annual meeting **of** shareholders or until their successors are elected are:

Name	Address

ARTICLE VII. All shareholders of the corporation shall be duly licensed to practice _____
under the laws of _____, and the original shareholders of the corporation are:

Name	Address

ARTICLE VIII. The following provisions are hereby adopted for the purpose of defining and regulating the authority of the corporation and of its stockholders, directors, and officers:

1. The original bylaws of the Corporation shall be the bylaws proposed and passed at the initial meeting of the incorporators and adopted by the board of directors. Additional bylaws and amendments to the current bylaws shall be voted upon at the annual meeting of stockholders; interim bylaws and amendments may be enacted by the board of directors, subject to ratification by the stockholders at the next annual meeting, but shall be in force until such ratification or rejection.

2. Any shareholder who for any reason shall have Corporation stock to sell shall offer these shares to all other shareholders and to the Corporation, at a price determined by the Stockholder Agreement, and shall accept any offer of purchase under such Agreement before offering the stock to persons outside the Corporation.

3. Unscheduled meetings of the Directors may be called without advance notice by any Director or Officer of the Corporation, provided that a quorum of Directors agrees to the meeting and signifies waiver of notice by attendance at the meeting.

4. Business of the Corporation may be conducted without calling a meeting, provided that the action is submitted in writing to a quorum of Directors, whose signature to the action shall constitute a waiver of meeting and the same approval as a vote cast in person at a regular meeting.

5. The Corporation alone shall hold the power to assign the duties and service of its employees, both regular and temporary, including employees substituting in an emergency or other unforeseen contingency.

ARTICLE IX. The duration of the corporation shall be ninety-nine (99) years.

We (I), the undersigned, being all the incorporators of the professional corporation identified above, declare that we have examined the foregoing this _____ day of _____ , 19_____ , and do declare it to be true and correct.

	Name	Address
(Signed)	_____	_____
	_____	_____
(Signed)	_____	_____
	_____	_____
(Signed)	_____	_____
	_____	_____

State of _____ , County of _____

THIS IS TO CERTIFY that on this date _____ before me, a notary public, personally appeared _____ , _____ and _____ who I am satisfied are the persons named as incorporators and executors of the foregoing Articles of Incorporation, and who by their respective signatures in my presence have acknowledged the same as their voluntary act.

IN TESTIMONY WHEREOF, I have hereunto set my hand and affixed my official seal on the date given above.

_____
Notary Public

My commission expires:

Initial State Filing Fees
For Professional Corporations

ALABAMA — *To the Probate Judge*

$1.00 per $1,000 of proposed capital stock — minimum $5.00 — No par valued at $100

$10.00 fee in advance for the filing of an incorporation statement with the Secretary of State

Recording Fee paid to Probate Judge at the rate of $.15 per 100 words of the certificate of incorporation plus $2.50 for examining certificate.

Total Minimum Fee — $17.80 plus $25.00 to Regulatory Board

ALASKA—*To Department of Commerce*

Authorized capital stock $100,000 or less — minimum is $25.00

No par stock valued at $1.00 per share

Total Minimum Fee — $25.00

ARIZONA—*To Corporation Commission*

Filing article of incorporation $50.00. Publication must be published in three newspapers of general circulation in the county where principal place of business.

Total Minimum Fee — $50.00

ARKANSAS — *To Secretary of State*

$15.00 minimum

($1.00 to $100,000 total capitalization)

No par — 1 share to 2,000 — $15.00 minimum

To County Clerk: for recording document $.25 plus $1.00 per page

Total Minimum Fee — $17.25

CALIFORNIA

$65.00 for filing Articles of Incorporation

$200.00 prepaid franchise tax

$15.00 for filing designation of agent

To County Recorder: $2.00 per instrument to clerk of county where principal place of business is

$3.00 to file statement by domestic corporation

Total Minimum Fee — $285.00

COLORADO — *To Secretary of State*

$22.50 for filing articles of incorporation (flat fee)

Total Minimum Fee — $22.50

CONNECTICUT — *To Secretary of State*

$1,000 stated capital

Franchise tax minimum fee is $50

Filing fee $20.00

Certified copy of incorporation $7.00 ($4.00 minimum), $3.00 affixing seal

Total Minimum Fee — $84.00

DELAWARE — *To Secretary of State*

No stated capital

$45.00 minimum filing fee

$8.00 to Recorder of Deeds

Total Minimum Fee — $53.00

DISTRICT OF COLUMBIA —

To Recorder of Deeds

$1,000 stated capital — Minimum $20.00 license fee

$20.00 articles of incorporation

$5.00 certified copy

$2.00 indexing

Total Minimum Fee — $53.50

FLORIDA — *To Secretary of State*

$30.00 minimum (not over $125,000 — $4.00 per $1,000)

$3.00 designation of agent

$15.00 Secretary of State permit fee

$15.00 certified copy

Total Minimum Fee — $78.00

GEORGIA — *To Secretary of State*

$500 stated capital

$15.00 for filing articles of incorporation — $.30 per page plus $1.00 for affixing seal

$15.00 publication fee

County Clerk — $.15 per 100 words plus $5.00 initial License tax — $10,000 or less $10.00 (tax based on net worth of company)

Total Minimum Fee — $52.50

HAWAII — *To Director of Regulatory Agencies of Hawaii $1,000 stated capital*

Articles of incorporation and affidavit of incorporation $.20 per $1,000 authorized capital stock $50.00 minimum, $1,000 maximum

Certification $.10 per page

Total Minimum Fee — $50.20

IDAHO — *To Secretary of State*

Minimum $20.00

No par $100 per share

Issuing certificate of incorporation $6.00

Affixing seal of state $1.00

County Recorder: filing, indorsing and indexing $1.00

Recording $.30

No par — $100 per share

Issuing certificate of incorporation— $6.00

Affixing seal of state — $1.00

County Recorder: filing, indorsing and indexing — $1.00

Recording — $.30

Total Minimum Fee — $28.30
(1,000 shares @ $.20 par value would apply to minimum tax of $20.00)
1,000 shares of no par value stock — $83.30

ILLINOIS — *To Secretary of State*

$1,000 stated capital

Filing fee $75.00

License fee $.50 minimum ($.50 per $1,000 stated capital)

Initial franchise tax $25.00

Certified copy $.50 per page plus $2.00 for affixing seal

Recording: $5.00 for first two pages, $1.00 for each additional page

Total Minimum Fee — $109.50

INDIANA — *To Secretary of State*

Minimum filing fee $30.00 (authorized shares of 1,000 or less) with or without par value

Designation of Agent $4.00

Certified copy $4.00, $2.00 for affixing seal

To County Recorder: $2.50 first page, $1.00 for each additional page

Total Minimum Fee — $47.50

IOWA — *To Secretary of State*

Filing certificate of incorporation $20.00

$.50 per page for Secretary of State to record & micro-film

To County Recorder:
$1.50 first page
$1.00 each additional page

Published within 3 months (between $10 and $15.00) one time in county of principal office

$1.00 to file publisher's affidavit with Secretary of State

Total Minimum Fee — $34.50

KANSAS — *To Secretary of State*

Application and recording fee $50

Certified copy $7.50 plus $1.00 per page

To Register of Deeds: 1st page $3.00, each additional page $1.00

Total Minimum Fee — $73.00

KENTUCKY — *To State Treasurer*
Organizational fee — minimum fee
— $10.00
Based on authorized stock up to
20,000 — $.01 per share
Secretary of State:
Articles of incorporation — $15
Certified copy — $.50 per page
plus $1.00 for seal
County Clerk: $5.00 for recording
first three legal pages — $1.00
each additional page
Total Minimum Fee — $34.00

LOUISIANA — *To Secretary of State*
Incorporation tax — $10.00 — if
exceeds total authorization of
$25,000 or 10,000 shares with-
out par value
Filing and recording articles of
incorporation — $5.00 plus $1.00
per page
Certified copy — $1.00 per page
plus $5.00 for seal
Total Minimum Fee — $31.00

MAINE — *To Secretary of State*
Up to $2 million—$10 per $100,000
Minimum fee is $10.00
Filing for articles of incorporation
$50.00
Secretary of State receiving service
of process $5.00
Certified copy — $1.00 per page
Total Minimum Fee — $69.00

MARYLAND — *State Department of
Assessments and Taxation*
Bonus tax based on authorized
stock up to $100,000 — $20.00
No par stock — $20.00
Recorded with Department of
Assessments and Taxation —
$15.00 plus $2.00 for each page
in excess of five
Total Minimum Fee — $35.00

MASSACHUSETTS — *To Secretary of
State*
Minimum fee $125.00
Certified copy of Incorporation —
$5.00
Total Minimum Fee — $135.00

MICHIGAN — *State of Michigan*
Minimum fee $25.00
Filing fee $10.00
Appointment of agent $5.00
Total Minimum Fee — $40.00

MINNESOTA — *To State Treasurer*
$1,000 stated capital
Minimum $62.50 for first $25,000
No par is $10.00
Published 21 days after Certificate
of Incorporation in county where
registered agent and office is
To Secretary of State — $12.50 for
articles of incorporation
Total Minimum Fee — $22.50

MISSISSIPPI — *To Secretary of State* —
$1,000 stated capital
Published within 30 days after cer-
tificate of incorporation is issued
Authorized stock $5,000 or less
$25.00
Certified copy $.60 per page and
$2.00 for seal (minimum fee is
$3.00)
Initial franchise tax — $10.00 must
be paid within sixty days after
incorporation
Total Minimum Fee — $41.40

MISSOURI — *To Director of Revenue*
$50.00 for first $30,000 of author-
ized stock
No par — $1.00 per share
Certified copy $1.50
Total Minimum Fee — $53.00

MONTANA — *Secretary of State*
Minimum fee — $50.00 license fee
No par — $1.00 per share
Filing article of incorporation —
$20.00
Certified copy of incorporation—
$.50 per page, $2.00 for seal
Total Minimum Fee — $73.00
(1,000 shares @ $.05 per share to
falls within minimum)

NEBRASKA — *To Secretary of State*
Published three successive weeks
Proof of publication filed with
the Secretary of State and office
of county clerk where registered
office is
Up to $10,000 — $20.00
Secretary of State $5.00 filing fee
and $2.00 per page for recording
Total Minimum Fee — $29.00

NEVADA — *To Secretary of State*
Initial fee $25.00 — no par $10.00
Certifying articles of incorporation
$5.00
County clerk — $2.50
$10.00 to file list of officers, direc-
tors and designation of registered
agent (must be filed within 60
days)
Total Minimum Fee — $27.50

NEW HAMPSHIRE — *Secretary of State*
Up to $15,000, fee is $60.00
No par — $50.00 per share for
first 20,000 shares
Total Minimum Fee — $60.00 (must
use par value and number of
shares of stock that equal $15,000
or less of total capitalization)

NEW JERSEY — *To Secretary of State*
(*Certified Checks Only*)

License fee is based on number of authorized shares; minimum fee is $25.00 — maximum fee $1000

Filing fee is $35.00 for certificate of incorporation

Certified copy is $10.00

No recording, no publication, no minimum capital required.

Total Minimum Fee — $80.00

NEW MEXICO — *State Corporation Commission*

Fee — $1.00 per $1,000.00 of authorized capital stock but no less than $50.00. Also, $10.00 minimum franchise tax is required at time certificate of incorporation is filed.

No par value stock is $1.00 per share

Certified copy is $.75 per page but not less than $10.00 plus $1.00 per page when Corporation Commission provides copies.

No minimum capital required

Total Minimum Fee — $70.00

NEW YORK — *Department of State*
(*Certified Checks Only*)

Certificate of Incorporation $50.00 (flat fee)

Photo fee is $10.00 and Certification is $.50 per page and $2.00 for certification and seal

Department of State transmits filed copy of certificate to county clerk for recording

Par value: initial authorized capital

1/20 of 1% — minimum: $10.00

No par value: $.05 per share—minimum $10.00

Total Minimum Fee — $76.00

NORTH CAROLINA—*Secretary of State*

Fees: Minimum is $45.00

Based on authorized capital stock $.40 per $1,000.00, minimum tax is $40.00 — maximum is $1,000.00

No par value stock is $1.00 per share

(a) Minimum tax: $40.00

(b) Filing fee $5.00 (flat fee for articles of incorporation)

Registrar of Deeds — $2.00 for 1st page plus $1.00 each additional page

Commissioner of Revenue: new corporations must file within 60 days of incorporation and pay minimum franchise tax $10.00

Total Minimum Fee — $58.00

NORTH DAKOTA — *Secretary of State*

Minimum Capital: $1,000.00

Initial License is based on authorized capital; par value up to $30,000 is $30.00. Over $30,000 is $30.00 plus $10.00 per $10,000 over $30,000

No par stock is $10.00 per share

Articles of incorporation and certificate is $20.00

Certified copy — $1.00 for every 4 pages plus $2.00 for seal and certification

Total Minimum Fee — $55.00

OHIO — *Secretary of State*

Articles of incorporation must state amount of capital with which the corporation will commence business but not less than $500.000

Initial fees based on number of shares of authorized capital stock for filing and recording articles of incorporation

0 to 1,000 is $.10 per share, 1,000 to 10,000 is $100.00, plus $.05 per share over 10,000, etc.

Total Minimum Fee — $50.00

OKLAHOMA — *Secretary of State*

Domestic corporations pay fee of $8.00 for filing articles of incorporation, plus $1.00 per $1,000 of authorized capital (minimum fee being $3.00). Also, a fee of $3.00 is assessed for filing affidavit of payment of amount of stated capital.

File certified copy with county clerk at fee of $5.00 plus $2.00 for each additional county in which required to be filed

Total Minimum Fee — $19.00

OREGON — *To Corporation Commissioner*

Domestic corporations pay organization fees based on authorized capital stock; $5,000 or less is $10.00, $5,000 to $10,000 is $15.00, $10,000 to $25,000 is $20.00, and increases accordingly. No par stock is valued at $10.00 per share.

Must pay annual license tax in advance at time of incorporation for the remainder of the first year of incorporation and follows fees of organization

Certified copy is $.50 per page and $2.00 for certificate and seal

Total Minimum Fee — $21.00

PENNSYLVANIA — *Commonwealth of Pennsylvania*

Must publish intent to file, or the filing of articles of incorporation once in general circulation of newspaper and once in legal newspaper.

No statutory minimum as the subscribed stock or paid-in capital before commencing business.

Domestic companies pay $75.00 for filing articles of incorporation, excise tax is payable at time of incorporation at rate of 12%

Certified copies of any document on file, fee is $1.00 per photocopy plus $7.50. Any other certificate is $10.00.

Total Minimum Fee — $92.00 plus 12% excise tax.

PUERTO RICO — *Secretary of State*

Fees payable in internal revenue stamps which are affixed to the documents and cancelled thereon, for filing articles of incorporation fees are based on authorized number of shares and minimum

fee is $100.00 without par value stock. With par value of $20,000 the fee is $.01 per share, $20,000 to $200,000 the fee is $200.00 plus $.005 per share in excess of 20,000 shares
Total Minimum Fee — $100.00

RHODE ISLAND — *Secretary of State*

Fees based on number of shares authorized with or without par value:

Up to 10,000 shares — $.01 per share not less than $80.00

10,000 to 100,000 shares — $100.00 plus $.005 per share in excess of 10,000 shares

Over 100,000 shares — $550.00 plus $.002 per share in excess

Articles of incorporation filing fee is $30.00

Certified copy is $.50 per page plus $2.00 for certificate and seal

No publication of charter required, no minimum capital requirement

Total Minimum Fee — $116.00

SOUTH CAROLINA — *Secretary of State*

Based on initial authorized capital (minimum $40.00)

$.40 per $1,000 of authorized capital

Filing articles of incorporation is $5.00

Stock issuance tax is $.10 of each $100 of face value or fraction thereof issued capital paid to Secretary of State

No par shares valued at $10.00 per share

Publication of Charter not required

Beginning capital must have minimum capitalization of $1,000.00 (at least $500 paid in cash)

No recording required

Total Minimum Fee — $51.30

SOUTH DAKOTA — *Secretary of State*

Initial fees based on authorized capital stock

(a) up to $25,000 — $40.00

(b) $25,000 to $100,000 — $60.00

(c) $100,000 to $500,000 — $80.00

(d) $500,000 to $1,000,000 — $100.00

(e) fees increase at the rate of $50.00 for $500,000 thereafter up to $5,000,000 and over — $500 plus $40.00 for each $500,000 of capital over $5,000,000

No par shares valued at $100 per share

Beginning capital is minimum capitalization of at least $1,000.00

No publication of charter and no recording required

Total Minimum Fee — $60.00

TENNESSEE — *Secretary of State*

Initial license fee is based on authorized capital

Par value shares (for the purpose of computing fees on par value stock each $100 unit of authorized stock is considered as a taxable share)

Up to 20,000 shares—$.01 per share

20,001 to 200,000 shares — $200 plus $.005 per share over 20,000

Over 200,000 shares — $1100 plus $.002 per share over 200,000 shares

No par shares up to 20,000 shares is $.01 per share

20,001 shares to 2,000,000 is $100 plus $.005 per share over 20,000

Over 2,000,000 shares is $5,050 plus $.002 per share over 2,000,000

※ Minimum fee par or no par is $10.00

✕ To County Registrar: recording any document is $5.00 plus $.50 for each or a part of a page in excess of 5 pages

No publication of charter required

Minimum capitalization is at least $1,000.00

Total Minimum Fee — $15.00

TEXAS — *Secretary of State*

Filing of articles of incorporation is $100.00 (flat fee)

Duplicate copies, original retained in his office, certified copy returned to incorporators

Beginning capital with minimum of $1,000.00

No publication of charter required

Secretary of State files and records certificate

Total Minimum Fee — $100.00

UTAH — *Secretary of State*

License fee based on authorized capital

Minimum fee is $25.00

No par stock valued at $1.00 rate of 1/20 of 1% of the dollar value of total authorized shares not less than $25.00 or more than $500.

Filing of articles of incorporation is $25.00

To State Tax Commission — upon incorporation, corporation must pre-pay $25.00 minimum franchise tax.

Filed and recorded in Secretary of State's office

Minimum capital is $1,000.00

Total Minimum Fee — $75.00

VERMONT — *Secretary of State*

Organization fee on the amount of authorized capital stock:

0 to $5,000 — fee is $20.00

$5,000 to $10,000 is $40.00

$10,000 to $50,000 is $80.00

$50,000 to $200,000 is $160.00

$200,000 to $500,000 is $320.00

File duplicate of Articles of Association (incorporation) Secretary of State retains original and returns certified copy to incorporators.

Certified copy is $.10 per page and $2.00 for affixing seal and cert.

No par value stock is assumed to have a par value of $100.00 per share.

Minimum tax is $20.00

No publication and no minimum capitalization required

Total Minimum Fee
  1000 no par — $164.40
  Minimum using par value — $24.40

VIRGINIA — *State Corporation Commission*

Domestic corporations pay a charter fee based on the maximum authorized capital at the following rates:

Up to $50,000 — $20.00

Over $50,000 but less than 3 million — $.40 per $1,000 or fraction thereof

No par value stock is valued at $100 per share

Also fee of $5.00 for filing Articles of Incorporation

Recording in Commission office is $1.00 per page or fee of $5.00 whichever is greater, and commission will forward to recorder of deeds in city or county of registered office, $1.00 for certification.

Certified copy is $.50 per page and $1.50 for seal.

Total Minimum Fee — $56.00

WASHINGTON — *Secretary of State*

File triplicate originals, original is retained in his office, one copy filed in the office of the county auditor in which the registered office is located and third copy is returned to incorporators.

Initial fee is based on authorized capital stock

Up to $50,000 — fee is $50.00

$50,000 to $1,000,000 is $50.00 plus 1/10 of 1% over $50,000

Minimum fee is $50.00 — Maximum is $5,000.00

Minimum capitalization is $500.00

Surtax is 25% and added to the original fees for filing Articles of Incorporation

An affidavit of incorporators stating value of assets received or to be received for no par value stock must accompany Articles of Incorporation

Certified copies — $5.00 per document plus $.50 per page for each 10 pages and $.25 for each additional page

Total Minimum Fee — $62.00 + 25% surtax

WEST VIRGINIA — *To Secretary of State*

License tax — up to $5,000 — $20
  $5,000 to $10,000 — $30

No par stock is valued at $25.00 per share

Filing Articles of Incorporation — $10.00

Clerk of County Court: $1.25 plus $.50 for each page over two for recording and indexing

Total Minimum Fee — $41.25

WISCONSIN — *To Secretary of State*

Filing Articles of Incorporation

$1.00 for each $1,000 or fraction of par value shares

$.02 for each share without par value

Minimum fee is $50.00

Register of Deeds: duplicate original marked filed by Secretary of State recorded in county of principal office — $.20 per folio

Minimum $1.50

Total Minimum Fee — $51.50

WYOMING — *Secretary of State*

$500.00 stated capital

Authorized capital stock up to $50,000 — fee $27.50

No par stock is valued at $1.00 per share

Total Minimum Fee — $27.50

Please note that all telephone calls and correspondence regarding the Professional Corporation Company Registered Agent services and any other inquiries should be addressed to:

Professional Corporation Co.
507 Beneficial Building
Wilmington, Delaware 19801

Phone: (302) 575-0440

Appendices

Appendix A

SUMMARY OF STATE
ENABLING LAWS

ALABAMA

Law and effective date: Professional Association Act: Ch. 16, Title 46, Code of Alabama, §§330-345. September 8, 1961, amended L. 1971, No. 184, effective July 30, 1971. Professional Corporation Act: Ch. 17, Title 46, Code of Alabama, §§346-366, effective February 10, 1972.

ALASKA

Law and effective date: AS §§10.45.010-10.45.260. Professional Corporation Act, effective April 24, 1968; amended by S.B. 45, L. 1969, effective August 4, 1969.

ARIZONA

Law and effective date: ARS §§10-901 through 10-909, March 20, 1962. Amendment of 1970 (L. 1970, C. 77), reducing to one the number required to form a corporation, effective July 14, 1970.

ARKANSAS

Laws and effective dates: AS §64-1701 et seq., The Medical Corporation Act, effective March 6, 1961; as amended through L. 1970, No. 13. AS §64-1801 et seq. The Dental Corporation Act, effective March 16, 1961. AS §64-2001 et seq., The Arkansas Professional Corporation Act, effective March 5, 1963.

CALIFORNIA

Laws and effective dates: Business and Professions Code §§1800-1808, Dental Corporations. Business and Professions Code §§2500-2503, Medical Corporations. Business and Professions Code §§6160-6172, Law Corporations. Corporations Code §§13400-13410, Professional Corporations. All foregoing effective November 13, 1968. Business and Professions Code §§2690-2696, Physical Therapy Corporations. Business and Professions Code

§§2995-2996.6, Psychological Corporations. Last two acts effective November 10, 1969. Business and Professions Code §§17875-17882, Marriage, Family, or Child Counseling Corporations. Effective March 7, 1973.

COLORADO

Laws and effective dates: Rule 265, Rules of Civil Procedure, Colorado Supreme Court, Professional Service Corporations, amended and effective August 20, 1970. (Authorizes formation of professional service corporations for the practice of law under the Colorado Corporations Code.) CRS (1973) §§12-36-117(1)(m) (practice of medicine); 12-36-134 (dentistry); 12-35-112 (veterinary medicine); 12-64-111(3) (attorneys). (All the foregoing sections of the Professional Service Corporation Act, effective July 1, 1969.) CRS (1973) §§12-32-109 & 12-41-125 authorize formation of professional service corporations by chiropodists and podiatrists and by physical therapists, effective June 11, 1973. §12-2-131, Public Accounting Corporation Act, effective April 1, 1970; §12-40-125, Optometric Corporations, effective March 29, 1973; §12-43-118, Psychology Corporations, effective June 25, 1973; §12-4-113, Architects.

CONNECTICUT

Laws and effective dates: CGSA §34-82, providing for Professional Associations, effective May 15, 1961. CGSA §§33-182 a-j, Professional Service Corporation Act, effective May 29, 1969, as amended by L. 1973, H.B. 9121, effective October 1, 1973.

DELAWARE

Law and effective date: Title 8 Delaware Code §§601-620, The Professional Service Corporation Act, effective June 7, 1969.

FLORIDA

Law and effective date: FSA §§621.02-621.15, The Professional Corporation Act, effective September 1, 1961. Amended by S.B. 1558, Laws of 1967, effective September 1, 1967, and by H.B. 1216, Laws of 1969, effective July 1, 1969.

GEORGIA

Laws and effective dates: GA. Code Ann. §84-4301 et seq., The Georgia Professional Association Act, effective April 5, 1961. Ch. 943, Laws 1970, Georgia Professional Corporation Act, effective March 11, 1970.

HAWAII

Law and effective date: HRS §§416-141 to 416-154, Professional Corporation Law, effective July 14, 1969.

IDAHO

Laws and effective dates: Idaho Code Ann. §§30-1301 to 30-1315, Professional Corporation Act, effective May 18, 1963. Amended by C. 182, Laws 1969, effective March 18, 1969, and by H.B. 407, Laws 1970. Idaho Code Ann. §54-1235, added by S. 43 effective February 15, 1963, permits professional engineers to practice through corporations.

ILLINOIS

Laws and effective dates: SHA ch. 106-1/2 §§101-110, Professional Association Act, effective August 9, 1961. SHA ch. 32 §§631-647, Medical Corporation Act, effective August 30, 1963. SHA ch. 32 §§415-1 to 415-17, The Professional Service Corporation Act, effective September 15, 1969, as amended by P.A. 77-565.

INDIANA

Laws and effective dates: IC 1971, §§23-1-14-1 to 23-1-14-21, Medical Professional Corporations, effective August 12, 1963. IC 1971, §§23-1-15-1 to 23-1-15-21, Dental Professional Corporations, *approved* March 8, 1965. Acts 1974, Ch. 13.5, Professional Accounting Corporations, effective July 1, 1974. IC 1971, §§23-1-13-1 to 23-1-13-11, Professional Corporations *approved* March 11, 1965. (Acts approved are effective upon proclamation by the governor.)

IOWA

Law and effective date: SF 554, L. 1970, Iowa Professional Corporation Act, effective July 1, 1970.

KANSAS

Law and effective date: KSA §§17-2706-17-2719, as amended by L. 1972, H.B. 1728. The Professional Corporation Law of Kansas, effective June 30, 1965. Secs. 17-2710 and 17-2711 amended by H.B. 1317, L. 1967, effective July 1, 1967, and by H.B. 1094, L. 1970, effective after publication.

KENTUCKY

Law and effective date: KRS §§274.005-274.990, Professional Service Corporation Act, effective June 15, 1962; as amended through L. 1972.

LOUISIANA

Laws and effective dates: RS §§12:801-12:815, Professional Law Corporations Act, effective July 29, 1964, as amended by Acts 1972, No. 78, No. 79, RS §§12:901-12:915, Professional Medical Corporation Act effective August 1, 1968, as amended by Acts 1972, No. 319, No. 134, RS §§12:981-12:995, Professional Dental Corporation Act, effective July 27, 1970, as amended by Acts 1972, No. 80, No. 127, RS §§12:1011-12:1025, Professional Accounting Corporation Act, effective July 29, 1970, as amended by Acts 1972, No. 82, No. 83.

MAINE

Law and effective date: MRSA, Title 13 §§701-716, The Professional Service Corporation Act, effective October 1, 1969.

MARYLAND

Law and effective date: ACM Art. 23 §§430-444, Professional Service Corporation Act, effective July 1, 1969; amended by Ch. 294, L. 1970, effective July 1, 1970.

MASSACHUSETTS

Law and effective date: GLM, CH. 156 A, Professional Corporations, effective November 17, 1963, as amended through L. 1973, (Ch. 367, effective July 9, 1973, and Ch. 478, effective July 30, 1973.)

MICHIGAN

Law and effective date: MSA §21-315(1) et seq., The Professional Service Corporation Act, effective March 28, 1963; amended through L. 1974, H.B. 4611, effective June 12, 1974.

MINNESOTA

Law and effective date: Minnesota Professional Corporation Act, by L. 1973, Ch. 40, effective March 22, 1973.

MISSISSIPPI

Law and effective date: MC §79-9-1 et seq., Professional Corporation Act, effective September 1, 1968; amended by H.B. 48, L. 1970, effective March 17, 1970, and by L. 1971, Ch. 332, effective March 6, 1971.

MISSOURI

Law and effective date: VAMS §§356.010-356.200, Professional Corporation Law, effective October 13, 1963, as amended by L. 1971, Act 117.

MONTANA

Law and effective date: RCM §15-2101 et seq., Professional Service Corporation Act, effective July 1, 1963; amended by H.B. 177, to include nurses, effective July 1, 1965; amended by S.B. 36, to include pharmacists and physical therapists, effective July 1, 1967.

NEBRASKA

Law and effective date: R.R.S. 1943 §§21-2201 to 21-2222, Professional Corporation Act, effective December 24, 1969.

NEVADA

Law and effective date: NRS 89.010-89.270, Professional Service Corporation Act, effective July 1, 1963; amended by S.B. 204, L. 1969, effective July 1, 1969, and by S.B. 217, L. 1969, effective April 16, 1969.

NEW HAMPSHIRE

Law and effective date: RSA §§294A:1 to 294A:8, Professional Associations, effective July 5, 1969.

NEW JERSEY

Law and effective date: NJSA 14A:17-1 through 17-18, Professional Service Corporation Act, effective December 16, 1969.

NEW MEXICO

Law and effective date: NMS §§51-22-1 to 51-22-13, Professional Corporation Act, effective July 1, 1963; amended by Ch. 245, L. 1969, effective April 3, 1969.

NEW YORK

Law and effective date: BCL, Art. 15, Professional Service Corporations, effective May 19, 1970.

NORTH CAROLINA

Law and effective date: GSNC, Ch. 55B, Professional Corporation Act, effective January 1, 1970, as amended by L. 1971, C. 196.

NORTH DAKOTA

Law and effective date: NDCC Ch. 10-31, Professional Corporation Act, effective July 1, 1963.

OHIO

Law and effective date: RC §1785.01 et seq., Professional Associations, effective

October 17, 1961; amended by H.B. 1, L. 1963, effective January 23, 1963.

OKLAHOMA
Law and effective date: 18 Okla. Stat. Ann. §801-819, Professional Corporation Act, effective July 26, 1961; amended by H.B. 768, L. 1963, effective June 18, 1963, by H.B. 769, L. 1963, effective June 24, 1963 by S.B. 502, L. 1970, effective March 30, 1970, by H.B. 1185, L. 1971, effective March 22, 1971 and by L. 1971, Ch. 164, effective May 25, 1971.

OREGON
Law and effective date: ORS §§58.005-.365, Professional Corporation Act, effective August 23, 1969, as amended by L. 1971, Ch. 362.

PENNSYLVANIA
Laws and effective dates: 15 P.S. §§12601-12619, Professional Association Act, effective August 7, 1961; 15 P.S. §§2901 to 2914, Professional Corporation Law, effective August 8, 1970.

RHODE ISLAND
Law and effective date: GL §§7-5.1-1 to 7-5.1-12, Professional Service Corporation Law, effective May 6, 1964, as amended by P.L. 1972, Ch. 100.

SOUTH CAROLINA
Law and effective date: CLSC §§56-1601 to 56-1617, Professional Association Act, effective March 22, 1962.

SOUTH DAKOTA
Laws and effective dates: SDCL §47-11-1 et seq., Medical Corporation Act, effective July 1, 1961; amended by H501, L. 1963, effective July 1, 1963. SDCL §47-11A-1 et seq., Chiropractic Corporation Act, SDCL 47-12-1 et seq., Dental Corporation Act, effective July 1, 1963. SDCL 47-13-1 et seq., Veterinary Corporation Act, effective July 1,

1964. SDCL 47-13A-1 et seq., as amended by L. 1973, H.B. 675, effective July 1, 1973, Professional Service Corporation for the Practice of Law, effective July 1, 1968. SDCL 47-13B-1 et seq., as amended by L. 1973, S.B. 118, effective July 1, 1973, Professional Corporations for the Practice of Public Accounting and S.B. 134, L. 1972.

TENNESSEE
Law and effective date: TCA §§48-2001 to 48-2007, Professional Corporation Act, effective February 18, 1970.

TEXAS
Laws and effective dates: VACS art. 1528e, Professional Corporation Act, effective January 1, 1970. VACS art. 1528f, Professional Association Act, effective June 18, 1969. VACS art. 6132b, §6, para. (3), Uniform Partnership Act, effective January 1, 1962.

UTAH
Law and effective date: UCA §§16-11-1 to 16-11-15, Professional Corporation Act, effective May 14, 1963, as amended by L. 1973, H.B. 143, effective May 8, 1973.

VERMONT
Law and effective date: VSA, T. 11 §§901-913, Professional Corporation Act, effective July 3, 1963.

VIRGINIA
Laws and effective dates: Code of Va. §§54-873 to 54-898, Professional Association Act, effective June 29, 1962; amended by Ch. 617, L. 1966, effective June 27, 1966, and by Ch. 28, L. 1968, effective June 28, 1968. Code of Va. §§13.1-542 to 13.1-566, Professional Corporation Act, effective June 26, 1970, as amended by L. 1972, Ch. 180.

WASHINGTON
Law and effective date: RCW Ch. 18.100, Professional Service Corporation Act, effec-

tive June 12, 1969, amended by H.B. 143, L. 1971, effective March 22, 1971.

WEST VIRGINIA

Laws and effective dates: W. Va. Code §§30-3-4b and c, Medical Corporations, effective June 12, 1965. W. Va. Code §§30-4-4b and c, Dental Corporations, effective March 10, 1967. W. Va. Code §30-2-5a, Legal Corporations. W. Va. Code §§30-14-9a and b, Osteopathic Physicians and Surgeons, effective March 6, 1973. W. Va. Code Sec. 30-10-18 and 19, Veterinary Medical Corporations, effective July 13, 1973. W. Va. Code Sec. 30-8-3a and b, and W. Va. Code Sec. 30-8-10, Optometric Corporations, effective July 13, 1973.

WISCONSIN

Law and effective date: WSA §180.99, The Service Corporation Law, effective August 11, 1961.

WYOMING

Law and effective date: §17-49.1 & 49.2. Ch. 34, Laws 1971, effective February 10, 1971. This Act permits incorporation under the Wyoming Business Corporation Act.

DISTRICT OF COLUMBIA

Law and effective date: §§29-1101 to 29-1119, District of Columbia Professional Corporation Act, approved December 10, 1971.

Appendix B

ADDRESSES FOR CORPORATION LAW, INFORMATION AND FORMS

ALABAMA
General Corporation Information
State of Alabama
Office of the Secretary of State
Montgomery, Alabama 36104
Forms:
The Michie Company
Law Publishers
Charlottesville, Virginia 22906

ALASKA
State of Alaska
Department of Commerce
Corporations
Pouch D
Juneau, Alaska 99811

ARIZONA
Arizona Corporation Division
2222 West Encanto Boulevard
Suite 210-D
Phoenix, Arizona 85009

ARKANSAS
Office of the Secretary of State
State of Arkansas
Corporation Department
Little Rock, Arkansas 72201

CALIFORNIA
Office of the Secretary of State
Corporate Division
111 Capitol Mall
Sacramento, California 95814

COLORADO
Office of the Secretary of State
Corporate Division
Daly Building, Third Floor
1576 Sherman
Denver, Colorado 80203

CONNECTICUT
Director, Corporations Division
Office of the Secretary of State
State of Connecticut
P.O. Box 846
30 Trinity Street
Hartford, Connecticut 06115

DELAWARE
State of Delaware
Department of State, Corporations
Townsend Building
P.O. Box 898
Dover, Delaware 19901

DISTRICT OF COLUMBIA
Recorder of Deeds of the
District of Columbia
Washington, D.C. 20005

FLORIDA
Chief, Bureau of Laws
Office of the Secretary of State
State of Florida
Capitol Building
Tallahassee, Florida 32304

GEORGIA
Corporation Commissioner
Office of the Secretary of State
214 State Capitol
Atlanta, Georgia 30334

HAWAII
General Corporation Information:
Department of Regulatory
Agencies
Business Registration Division
P.O. Box 40
Honolulu, Hawaii 96810

Professional Corporation Details:
Corporation and Securities
Administrator
Professional and Vocational
Licensing
P.O. Box 3469
Honolulu, Hawaii 96810

IDAHO

State of Idaho
Secretary of State
Boise, Idaho 83707

ILLINOIS

Secretary of State
Springfield, Illinois 62756

INDIANA

Office of the Secretary of State
Corporations Division
201 State House
Indianapolis, Indiana 46204

IOWA

Secretary of State
State Capitol
Des Moines, Iowa 50319

KANSAS

State of Kansas
Office of the Secretary of State
Topeka, Kansas 66612

KENTUCKY

Secretary of State's Office
State Capitol Building
Frankfort, Kentucky 40601

LOUISIANA

State of Louisiana
Secretary of State
P.O. Box 44125
Baton Rouge, Louisiana 70804

MAINE

Secretary of State
Augusta, Maine 04330

MARYLAND

State Department of Assessments
and Taxation
301 West Preston Street
Baltimore, Maryland 21201

MASSACHUSETTS

The Commonwealth of Massachusetts
Office of the Secretary of the
Commonwealth
Corporations Division
State House
Boston, Massachusetts 02133

MICHIGAN

State of Michigan
Department of Commerce
Corporation Division
P.O. Drawer C
Lansing, Michigan 48904

MINNESOTA

State of Minnesota
Office of the Secretary of State
Corporate Division
St. Paul, Minnesota 55155

MISSISSIPPI

Secretary of State
Jackson, Mississippi 39205

MISSOURI

State of Missouri
Office of the Secretary of State
Jefferson City, Missouri 65101

MONTANA

State of Montana
Office of the Secretary of State
Helena, Montana 59601

NEBRASKA
Nebraska Department of State
Secretary of State
Lincoln, Nebraska 68509

NEVADA
Secretary of State
Carson City, Nevada 89701

NEW HAMPSHIRE
The State of New Hampshire
Secretary of State
State House
Concord, New Hampshire 03300

NEW JERSEY
State of New Jersey
Department of State
Trenton, New Jersey 08625

NEW MEXICO
State of New Mexico
State Corporation Commission
Corporation and Franchise
    Tax Departments
Santa Fe, New Mexico 87501

NEW YORK
The University of the State of New York
The State Education Department
Division of Professional Licensing
99 Washington Avenue
Albany, New York 12210

NORTH CAROLINA
State of North Carolina
Department of the Secretary of State
Raleigh, North Carolina 27603

NORTH DAKOTA
Secretary of State
Bismarck, North Dakota 58505

OHIO
Secretary of State
Columbus, Ohio 43216

OKLAHOMA
Secretary of State
Oklahoma State Capitol
Oklahoma City, Oklahoma 73105

OREGON
Department of Commerce
Commerce Department
Commerce Building
Salem, Oregon 97310

PENNSYLVANIA
General Corporation Information:
    Pennsylvania Office of the
        Secretary of the Commonwealth
    Harrisburg, Pennsylvania 17120
Forms:
    All-state Legal Supply
        Corporation
    1316 Arch Street
    Philadelphia, Pennsylvania 19107

RHODE ISLAND
Department of State
Secretary of State
Providence, Rhode Island 02903

SOUTH CAROLINA
State of South Carolina
Department of State
P.O. Box 11350
Columbia, South Carolina 29211

SOUTH DAKOTA
State of South Dakota
Department of State
Pierre, South Dakota 57501

TENNESSEE
State of Tennessee
Office of the Secretary of State
Corporations Department
Nashville, Tennessee 37219

TEXAS

Deputy Director, Corporation Division
State of Texas
Office of the Secretary of State
Austin, Texas 78711

UTAH

Secretary of State
203 State Capitol Building
Salt Lake City, Utah 84114

VERMONT

State of Vermont
Secretary of State
Montpelier, Vermont 05602

VIRGINIA

General Corporation Information:
State Corporation Commission
Box 1197
Richmond, Virginia 23209
Forms:
The Michie Company
Law Publishers
Charlottesville, Virginia 22906

WASHINGTON

Secretary of State
Olympia, Washington 98504

WEST VIRGINIA

State of West Virginia
Office of the Secretary of State
Corporation Division
Charleston, West Virginia 25305

WISCONSIN

State of Wisconsin
Department of State
State Capitol
Madison, Wisconsin 53702

WYOMING

Secretary of State
State Capitol
Cheyenne, Wyoming 82002

Appendix C

SPECIMEN FORM FOR PROFESSIONAL
CORPORATION BYLAWS

The following is a sample set of bylaws for a professional corporation.* They were initially designed for Missouri but can be used in other states with a minimum of adapting.

Bylaws of a Professional Corporation
Article I: Offices

The principal office of the corporation in the State of Missouri shall be located in _____, Missouri. The corporation may have such other offices, either within or without the State of Missouri, as the business of the corporation may require from time to time.

The registered office of the corporation required to be maintained in the State of Missouri, may be, but need not be, identical with the principal office in the State of Missouri, and the address of the registered office may be changed from time to time by the Board of Directors.

Article II: Shareholders

Section 1. Annual Meeting: The annual meeting of the Shareholders shall be held at the hour of _____ in each year beginning with the year _____ for the purpose of electing Directors and for the transaction of such other business as may come before the meeting. If the day fixed for the annual meeting shall be a legal holiday, such meeting shall be held on the next succeeding business day. If the election of Directors shall not be held on the day designated herein for any annual meeting, or at any adjournment thereof, the Board of Directors shall cause the election to be held at a special meeting of the Shareholders as soon thereafter as conveniently may be.

Section 2. Special Meetings: Special meetings of the Shareholders may be called by the President, by the Board of Directors or by the holders of not less than one-fifth of all the outstanding shares of the corporation.

Section 3. Place of Meeting: The Board of Directors may designate any place, either within or without the State of Missouri, as the place of meeting for any annual meeting of the Shareholders or for any special meeting of the Shareholders called by the Board of Directors. The Shareholders may designate any place, either within or without the State of Missouri, as the place for the holding of such meeting, and may include the same in a waiver of notice of any meeting. If no designation is made, or if a special meeting be otherwise called, the place of meeting shall be the registered office of the corporation in the State of Missouri, except as otherwise provided in Section 5 of this Article.

Section 4. Notice of Meetings: Written or printed notice stating the place, day and hour of the meeting and, in case of a special meeting, the purpose or purposes for which the meeting is called, shall be delivered not less than ten nor more than fifty (50) days before the date of the meeting, either personally or by mail, by or at the direction of the President, or the Secretary, or the officer or persons calling the meeting, to each Shareholder of record entitled to vote at such meeting. If mailed, such notice shall be deemed to be delivered when deposited in the United States mail in a sealed envelope addressed to the Shareholder at his address as it appears on the records of the corporation, with postage thereon

---

*Specimen form for bylaws, minutes, employment agreement and shareholders agreement reprinted by permission from publisher of Professional Corporation Desk Book; Institute for Business Planning, Inc., 13P Plaza, Englewood Cliffs, N.J. 07632.

prepaid. In addition, to the written or printed notice, a notice of the place, day and hour of the meeting shall be published in a daily or weekly newspaper published in the City or County where the registered office of the corporation is located, the first insertion to be not less than ten days prior to the date of the meeting, and if such notice be published in a weekly newspaper, such notice shall be published at least twice, and if such notice be published in a daily newspaper, such notice shall be published at least nine times.

Section 5. Meeting of All Shareholders: If all of the Shareholders shall meet at any time and place, either within or without the State of Missouri, and consent to the holding of a meeting, such meeting shall be valid, without call or notice, and at such meeting any corporate action may be taken.

Section 6. Voting Lists: The original share ledger or transfer book, or a duplicate thereof kept in this state, shall be prima facie evidence as to who are the Shareholders entitled to vote at any meeting of Shareholders.

Section 7. Quorum: A majority of the outstanding shares of the corporation, represented in person or by proxy, shall constitute a quorum at any meeting of the Shareholders; provided, that if less than a majority of the outstanding shares are represented at said meeting, a majority of the shares so represented may adjourn the meeting, from time to time, without further notice, to a date not longer than ninety days from the date originally set for such meeting.

Section 8. Proxies: At all meetings of Shareholders, a Shareholder may vote by proxy granted to another Shareholder only executed in writing by the Shareholder or by his duly authorized attorney-in-fact; provided, however, all proxies are subject to the provisions of Sec. 356.070 R.S. Mo. Such proxy shall be filed with the Secretary of the Corporation before or at the time of the meeting. No proxy shall be valid after eleven months from the date of its execution, unless otherwise provided in the proxy.

Section 9. Voting of Shares: Subject to the provisions of Section 12, each outstanding share of capital stock having voting rights shall be entitled to one vote upon each matter submitted to a vote at a meeting of Shareholders.

Section 10. Voting of Shares by Certain Holders: Shares standing in the name of an unqualified or ineligible Shareholder, as defined by The Professional Corporation Law of Missouri, shall not be entitled to vote.

A Shareholder whose shares are either pledged or held as collateral security shall be entitled to vote such shares until the shares have been transferred into the name of the pledgee, and thereafter the pledgee shall not be entitled to vote the shares so transferred but shall hold such shares as an ineligible and unqualified person as defined by The Professional Corporation Law of Missouri.

Section 11. Cumulative Voting: Cumulative voting shall not be allowed except in the election of Directors.

Section 12. Informal Action by Shareholders: Any action which may be taken at the meeting of the Shareholders may be taken without a meeting if a consent in writing, setting forth the action so taken, shall be signed by all of the Shareholders entitled to vote with respect to the subject matter thereof.

Article III: Directors

Section 1. General Powers: No person may be a Director of the corporation unless he is a Shareholder and the business and affairs of the corporation shall be managed by its Board of Directors.

Section 2. Number, Election and Term: The number of Directors of the corporation shall be _____, each of whom must be a Shareholder, who shall be elected at the first annual meeting of the Shareholders, and annually thereafter, for a term of one year, and each of whom shall hold office until his successor has been elected and has qualified.

Section 3. Regular Meetings: A regular meeting of the Board of Directors shall be held without other notice than this Bylaw, immediately after, and at the same place as, the annual meeting of Shareholders. The Board of Directors may provide, by resolution, the time and place, either within or without the State of Missouri, for the holding of additional regular meetings with notice of such resolution to all Directors.

Section 4. Special Meetings: Special meetings of the Board of Directors may be called by or at the request of the President or any two Directors. The person or persons authorized to call special meetings of the Board of Directors may fix any place in the United States, either within or without the State of Missouri, as the place for holding any special meeting of the Board of Directors called by them.

Section 5. Notice: Notice of any special meeting shall be given at least five days previously thereto by written notice delivered personally or mailed to each Director at his business address or by telegram provided, however, that if the designated meeting place is without the State of Missouri, an additional five days' notice shall be given. If mailed, such notice shall be deemed to be delivered when deposited in the United States mail in a sealed envelope so addressed, with postage thereon prepaid. If notice be given by telegram, such notice shall be deemed to be delivered when the telegram is delivered to the telegraph company. Any Director may waive notice of any meeting. The attendance of a Director at any meeting shall constitute a waiver of notice of such meeting, except where a Director attends a meeting for the express purpose of objecting to the transaction of any business because the meeting is not lawfully called or convened. Neither the business to be transacted at, nor the purpose of, any regular or special meeting of the Board of Directors need be specified in the notice or waiver of notice of such meeting.

Section 6. Quorum: A majority of the Board of Directors shall constitute a quorum for the transaction of business at any meeting of the Board of Directors, provided that if less than a majority of the Directors are present at said meeting, a majority of the Directors present may adjourn the meeting from time to time without further notice.

Section 7. Manner of Acting: The act of the majority of the Directors present at a meeting of the Directors at which a quorum is present shall be the act of the Board of Directors.

Section 8. Vacancies: In case of the death or resignation or disqualification of one or more of the Directors, a majority of the survivors or remaining Directors may fill such vacancy or vacancies, only from other Shareholders of the corporation, until the successor or successors are elected at the next annual meeting of the Shareholders. A Director elected to fill a vacancy shall serve as such until the next annual meeting of the Shareholders.

Section 9. Compensation: Directors as such shall not receive any stated salaries for their services, but by resolution of the Board of Directors, a fixed sum and expenses of attendance, if any, may be allowed for attendance at each regular or special meeting of the Board of Directors; provided, that nothing herein contained shall be construed to preclude any Director from serving the corporation in any other capacity and receiving compensation therefor.

Section 10. Executive Committee: The Board of Directors may authorize and designate from time to time or on a regular basis three (3) Directors to constitute an Executive Committee which shall have and exercise all powers of the Board of Directors in the management of the corporation.

Article IV: Officers

Section 1. Number and Qualification: No person may be an officer, other than Secretary, unless he is a Shareholder. If the number of Shareholders is less than three, the officers may be President and Secretary only. Any two or more offices may be held by the same person, except the offices of President and Secretary.

All officers of the corporation, as between themselves and the corporation, shall have such authority and perform such duties in the management of the property and affairs of the corporation as may be provided in the Bylaws, or, in the absence of such provision, as may be determined by resolution of the Board of Directors.

Section 2. Election and Term of Office: The officers of the corporation shall be elected annually by the Board of Directors at the first meeting of the Board of Directors held after each annual meeting of Shareholders. If the election of officers shall not be held at such meeting, such election shall be held as soon thereafter as conveniently may be. Each officer shall hold office until his successor shall have been duly elected and shall have qualified or until his death or until he shall resign or shall have been removed in the manner hereinafter provided.

Section 3. Removal: Any officer elected or appointed by the Board of Directors may be removed by the Board of Directors whenever such officer becomes either ineligible or disqualified as a Shareholder under The Professional Corporation Law of Missouri or in the judgment of the Board of Directors the best interests of the corporation would be served thereby, but such removal shall be without prejudice to the contract rights, if any, of the person so removed.

Section 4. Vacancies: If the office of any officer of the corporation becomes vacant because of death, resignation, removal, disqualification or for any other reason or if any officer of the corporation is unable to perform the duties of his office for any reason, the Board of Directors may choose a successor who shall replace such officer or the Board of Directors may delegate the duties of any such vacant office to any other officer or to any director of the corporation for the unexpired portion of the term.

Section 5. President: The President must be a Shareholder and shall be the principal executive officer of the corporation and shall in general supervise and control all of the business and affairs of the corporation. He shall preside at all meetings of the Shareholders and of the Board of Directors. He may sign, with the Secretary or any other proper officer thereunto authorized by the Board of Directors, certificates for shares of the corporation, any deeds, mortgages, bonds, contracts or other instruments which the Board of Directors have authorized to be executed, except in cases where the signing and execution thereof shall be expressly delegated by the Board of Directors or by these Bylaws to some other officer or agent of the corporation, or shall be required by law to be otherwise signed or executed; and in general shall perform all duties incident to the office of President and such other duties as may be prescribed by the Board of Directors from time to time.

Section 6. Vice-Presidents: In the absence of the President or in the event of his inability or refusal to act, the Vice-President who must be a Shareholder (or in the event there be more than one Vice-President, the Vice-Presidents, all of whom must be Shareholders, in the order of their election) shall perform the duties of the President, and when so acting, shall have all the powers of and be subject to all the restrictions upon the President. Any Vice-President may sign, with the Secretary, certificates for shares of the corporation; and shall perform such other duties as from time to time may be assigned to him by the President or by the Board of Directors.

Section 7. The Treasurer: If required by the Board of Directors, the Treasurer, who must be a Shareholder, shall give a bond for the faithful discharge of his duties in such sum and with such surety or sureties as the Board of Directors shall determine. He shall: (a) have charge and custody of and be responsible for all funds and securities of the corporation; receive and give receipts for moneys due and payable to the corporation from any source whatsoever, and deposit all such moneys in the name of the corporation in such banks, trust companies or other depositaries as shall be selected in accordance with the provisions of Article V of these Bylaws: (b) in general perform all the duties incident to the office of Treasurer and such other duties as from time to time may be assigned to him by the President or by the Board of Directors.

Section 8. Secretary: The Secretary, who need not be a Shareholder, shall: (a) keep the minutes of the Shareholders' and of the Board of Directors' meetings in one or more books provided for that purpose; (b) see that all notices are duly given in accordance with the provisions of these Bylaws or as required by law; (c) be custodian of the corporate records and of the seal of the corporation and see that the seal of the corporation is affixed to all certificates for shares prior to the issue thereof and to all documents, the execution of which on behalf of the corporation under its seal is duly authorized in accordance with the provisions of these Bylaws; (d) keep a register of the post office address of each Shareholder which shall be furnished to the Secretary by such Shareholder; (e) sign with the President, or a Vice-President, certificates for shares of the corporation, the issue of which shall have been authorized by resolution of the Board of Directors; (f) have general charge of the stock transfer books of the corporation; (g) in general perform all duties incident to the office of Secretary and such other duties as from time to time may be assigned to him by the President or by the Board of Directors.

Section 9. Salaries: The salaries of the officers shall be fixed from time to time by the Board of Directors and no officer shall be prevented from receiving such salary by reason of the fact that he is also a Director of the corporation.

Article V: Contracts, Loans, Checks and Deposits

Section 1. Contracts: The Board of Directors may authorize any officer or officers, to enter into any contract or execute and deliver any instrument in the name of and on behalf of the corporation, and such authority may be general or confined to specific instances.

Section 2. Loans: No loans shall be contracted on behalf of the corporation and no evidences of indebtedness shall be issued in its name unless authorized by a resolution of the Board of Directors. Such authority may be general or confined to specific instances.

Section 3. Checks, Drafts, etc.: All checks, drafts or other orders for the payment of money, notes or other evidences of indebtedness issued in the name of the corporation, shall be signed by such officer or officers, agent or agents of the corporation and in such manner as shall from time to time be determined by resolution of the Board of Directors.

Section 4. Deposits: All funds of the corporation not otherwise employed shall be deposited from time to time to the credit of the corporation in such banks, trust companies, or other depositaries as the Board of Directors may select.

Article VI: Certificates for
Shares and Their Transfer

Section 1: Certificates for Shares: Certificates representing shares of the corporation shall be in such form as may be determined by the Board of Directors. Such certificates shall be signed, manually or by facsimile or otherwise, by the President or Vice-President and by the Secretary, and shall be sealed with the seal of the corporation. All certificates for shares shall be consecutively numbered and shall contain either in the body of the certificate or by appropriate legend appearing as part of the certificate that such shares are issued subject to all the limitations and qualifications of The Professional Corporation Law of Missouri. The name of the person owning the shares represented thereby with the number of shares and date of issue shall be entered on the books of the corporation. All certificates surrendered to the corporation for transfer shall be cancelled and no new certificate shall be issued until the former certificate for a like number of shares shall have been surrendered and cancelled, except that in case of a lost, destroyed or mutilated certificate a new one may be issued therefor upon such terms and indemnity to the corporation as the Board of Directors may prescribe.

Section 2. Transfers of Shares: A Shareholder may voluntarily transfer his shares to the corporation or to a qualified person with the prior written consent of the corporation. No shares may be transferred upon the books of the corporation or issued by the corporation until there is presented to and filed with the corporation a certificate by the regulating board stating that the person to whom the transfer is to be made or the shares issued is duly licensed to render the same type of professional services as that for which the corporation was organized. No Shareholder shall enter into any voting trust agreement, proxy, or any other type of agreement vesting another person, other than another Shareholder of the same corporation, with authority to exercise the voting power of any or all of his stock. The issuance or transfer of any shares and any proxy, voting trust or other agreement made in violation of this section shall be null and void.

Section 3. Treasury Stock: All issued and outstanding stock of the corporation that may be purchased or otherwise acquired by the corporation shall be treasury stock, and shall be subject to disposal by action of the Board of Directors. Such stock shall neither vote nor participate in dividends while held by the corporation.

Article VII: Fiscal Year
The fiscal year of the corporation shall begin on the first day of _____ in each year and end on the last day of _____ in each year.

Article VIII: Dividends
The Board of Directors may from time to time, declare, and the corporation may pay, dividends on its outstanding shares in the manner and upon the terms and conditions provided by law and its Articles of Incorporation.

Article IX: Seal
The corporation shall have a corporate seal which shall have inscribed around the circumference thereof "_____, Missouri," and elsewhere thereon shall bear the words "Corporate Seal." The corporate seal may be affixed by impression or may be by facsimile.

Article X: Waiver of Notice
Whenever any notice whatever is required to be given under the provisions of these Bylaws or under the provisions of the Articles of Incorporation or under the provisions of The Professional Corporation Law of Missouri, waiver thereof in writing, signed by the person or persons entitled to such notice, whether before or after the time stated therein, shall be deemed equivalent to the giving of such notice.

Article XI: Indemnification of Officers
and Directors Against Liabilities
and Expenses in Actions
Each Director or officer, or former Director or officer of this corporation, and his legal representatives, shall be indemnified by this corporation against liabilities, expenses, counsel fees and costs reasonably incurred by him or his estate in connection with, or arising out of, any action, suit, proceeding or claim in which he is made a party by reason of his being, or having been, such Director or officer but nothing in this Article or these Bylaws shall restrict or limit in any manner the authority and duty of any regulating board for the licensing of individual persons rendering professional service or the practice of the profession which is within the jurisdiction of the regulating board, notwithstanding that the person is an officer, director, Shareholder or employee of the corporation and rendering professional service or engaging in the practice of the profession through the corporation.

Article XII: Amendments
These Bylaws may be altered, amended or repealed and new Bylaws may be adopted at any annual meeting of the Shareholders or at any special meeting of the Shareholders called for that

purpose. The Board of Directors may adopt emergency Bylaws as provided by Law.

Adopted this _____ day of _____, 19 _____;

_____

Attest:

_____

SPECIMEN MINUTES OF BOARD OF DIRECTORS

The following is a sample set of minutes of the first meeting of the board of directors of a professional corporation. Note that the shareholders are authorized to elect officers. In most states that allow shareholders to elect officers, authorization must be made in the certificate of incorporation.

Minutes of First Meeting of Board of Directors
(Name of professional corporation)

The first meeting of the board of directors of _____ _____ was held on _____ at the corporation's offices at _____ _____.

The following directors being a quorum and all of the directors of the corporation were present

(list of directors)

_____

_____

_____

_____ was nominated and elected chairman of the board and acted as chairman of the organization meeting.

_____ was nominated and elected secretary of the board of directors and acted as secretary of the meeting.

After presentation by the chairman and discussion by the directors the following resolutions were adopted being made by _____, seconded by _____.

RESOLVED that the share and transfer book presented by the chairman of this meeting at the organization meeting is adopted as the share and transfer book of the corporation.

Upon the motion of _____, seconded by _____ and unanimously approved it was:

RESOLVED that the president and the secretary of the corporation are authorized to issue certificates for the shares in the form submitted to the organization meeting by the chairman and appended to the minutes of the meeting.

Upon the motion of _____, seconded by _____ and unanimously approved it was:

RESOLVED that the board of directors for professional corporation shall consist of _____ directors to be elected by the shareholders of the corporation.

An offer was made by _____ and (original shareholders) who have previously conducted business as partners in a partnership engaged in the practice of (profession) to each _____ subscribe to _____ shares of the authorized capital stock of the professional corporation in exchange for the assignment effective as of _____ to the corporation of their interests in the partnership and all of the assets subject to all of the liabilities of the partnership. Upon motion made by _____, seconded by _____ and unanimously approved it was:

RESOLVED that the offer and subscription of (original shareholders) doing business as partners in the practice of (profession) to each acquire (number) shares of no par value common stock of professional corporation_____
in consideration and exchange for the assignment effective as of the close of business on (date of transfer) to this corporation of their interest in their partnership in all the assets, subject to all the liabilities of their partnership as a going business including accounts receivables, but excluding cash pursuant to the form of agreement considered at this meeting is accepted and the proper officers are authorized and directed to execute the assignment agreement for this corporation and to issue a certificate for shares of stock to each in accordance with the terms of the assignment agreement.

The chairman then presented a copy of a lease covering the office space leased by the partnership in which the predecessor partnership carried on its business. Upon a motion made by _____, seconded by _____ _____ and unanimously approved it was:

RESOLVED that the president of the professional corporation is authorized and directed on behalf of the corporation to assume the lease, or to negotiate and execute a new lease for the corporation's offices located at _____

_____

_____.

The chairman then indicated that certain expenses have been incurred in connection with the organization and formation of the corporation. Upon a motion made by _____ _____, seconded by _____ and unanimously approved it was:

RESOLVED that the Treasurer of this professional corporation is authorized to pay all charges and expenses incidental to or arising out of the organization of this professional corporation and to reimburse any person who has made any payment or disbursement for that purpose.

Upon motion of _____ and seconded by _____ and unanimously approved it was:

RESOLVED that this professional corporation proceed to carry on the profession for which it was incorporated.

The chairman indicated that for the corporation to carry on the practice of (profession) it was essential that it employ licensed (professionals). He submitted prepared forms of employment agreements between the corporation and _____,

_____, _____and

_____. Upon motion made by _____

_____ and seconded by _____ and unanimously approved, it was:

RESOLVED that the proposed employment agreements with _____

_____, _____,

_____ and _____

are hereby accepted and that the president or other officer designated by the president is authorized and directed to execute the employment agreements for the corporation and that the secretary be directed to affix the corporate seal to the employment agreements, and be it further

RESOLVED that a copy of each employment agreement be appended to the minutes of the meeting.

The chairman also indicated that it was advantageous for the professional corporation to provide a deferred compensation plan under which the employees of the corporation would continue as consultants subsequent to the termination of their employment.

The chairman presented a proposed resolution to the meeting. Upon the motion made by _____, seconded by _____ _____, it was unanimously

RESOLVED that the officers of the corporation be retained as consultants in the practice of _____ by the corporation after the termination of their active employment on the terms, conditions and provisions contained in the proposed agreement which has been submitted to this meeting by the chairman (a copy of the proposed plan is attached to the minutes herein) and that the officers of the corporation are authorized and directed to execute the employment agreement on behalf of the corporation.

The chairman of the meeting also suggested that the corporation and the shareholders enter into an agreement providing for purchase and sale of stock in the corporation and restrictions on the transfer of the shares of stock of the corporation. The chairman presented a proposed form of an agreement between the corporation and the shareholders restricting the transfer of shares and providing for the sale of securities in the event of a shareholder's retirement or disability. Upon the motion of _____, seconded by _____ _____ and unanimously approved, it was:

RESOLVED that the restrictive stock transfer agreement submitted to the directors by the chairman of the meeting is hereby approved and that the directors of the corporation be authorized and directed to execute it for the corporation.

The chairman presented a form of bank resolution authorizing the establishment of an account with the _____Bank. Upon the motion of _____, seconded by _____ and unanimously approved by the directors it was:

RESOLVED that any _____ of the following named persons, or persons from time to time holding the following offices of this corporation

_____

_____

_____

be and they hereby are authorized to arrange for the borrowing of and to borrow from time to time from _____ Bank such sums upon such terms and conditions as to time of repayment, rate of interest and security therefore as they may determine; and that they be and hereby are authorized to execute and deliver in the name and on behalf of this corporation promissory notes in evidence of the obligations of repayment with respect to all sums so borrowed; to pledge or assign property of this corporation to said Bank as security for such borrowings, and to execute and deliver security agreements of all kinds and any and all other instruments whether of obligation or hypothecation which they may determine necessary or appropriate in implementation of the borrowing authority hereby conferred.

RESOLVED that the secretary or clerk of this corporation be and hereby is authorized and directed to certify to _____ Bank the foregoing resolution or resolutions and that the provisions thereof are in conformity with the charter and bylaws of this corporation and that the foregoing resolutions and the authority thereby conferred shall remain in full force and effect until this corporation officially notifies said Bank to the contrary in writing and said Bank may conclusively presume that such resolves are in effect and that the persons identified from time to time as officers of the corporation by certificate of the clerk or secretary have been duly elected or appointed to and continue to hold such offices.

I further certify that the present officers of said corporation duly elected or appointed to hold office until their respective successors are chosen, and empowered to act for and on behalf of this corporation in any of its business with said Bank within the authority prescribed in the foregoing resolution or resolutions certified to said bank, are:

Name_____ Title_____

SPECIMEN EMPLOYMENT AGREEMENT

AGREEMENT made this the _____ day of _____,
19_____ by and between (name of professional corporation) (hereinafter sometimes known as
GREEN & BROWN), a professional corporation incorporated under and existing by virtue of the
Professional Corporation Laws of the State of _____,
having its principal place of business at _____
and (name of professional) a duly licensed (profession) residing at (residence address of the professional)
(hereinafter sometimes known as BROWN).

IN CONSIDERATION OF ONE DOLLAR AND OTHER GOOD AND VALU-
ABLE CONSIDERATION, be it agreed:

First: Term: BROWN agrees to faithfully serve GREEN & BROWN in the practice of
_____ (hereinafter referred
to as Practice) until the employment relationship is terminated as provided for herein.

Second: Duties: BROWN agrees to devote full time and attention to the performance of
professional services in the practice of _____ and the additional
time that may be required of him for the administration and management of GREEN & BROWN. His
duty schedule shall be determined by the officers and directors of GREEN & BROWN. BROWN will
not engage in any outside professional activities involving financial return without GREEN & BROWN's
written consent.

BROWN shall provide such emergency evening and weekend coverage of the Practice
as shall be reasonably assigned to him by GREEN & BROWN.

(Editor's Note: A clause such as this should be used where the practice is apt to involve
weekend and emergency work, such as in the case of physicians.)

Third: Salary: BROWN shall receive and GREEN & BROWN shall pay him during the
term of this Agreement salary at the rate of $30,000 per year, payable in monthly payments.

(Editor's Note: A professional's salary from a professional corporation is subject to
Social Security, Federal income tax withholding and other employment taxes.)

Fourth: Additional Compensation: In addition to the salary provided for above, GREEN
& BROWN shall institute the following additional compensation programs:

(A) A qualified employee profit-sharing plan containing provisions for. retirement,
disability and death benefits that may be provided for employees within the maximum permissible
limitations for qualified retirement plans under the Internal Revenue Code; substantially in the form
set forth as Exhibit A attached hereto and included herein as if said Agreement and trust were set
forth herein.

(B) An employees' group life insurance plan to provide group life insurance as permitted
by Section 79 of the Internal Revenue Code or any amendments thereto.

(C) An accident and health plan for the reimbursement or payment of medical
care expenses.

(D) A disability plan for the payment of disability benefits as permitted under the
Internal Revenue Code.

(E) If BROWN dies during the term of this Agreement, BROWN & GREEN shall pay
to his named beneficiary or in the event BROWN has not named a beneficiary or his named beneficiary is
deceased, his estate, all salary accrued by and unpaid at the date of BROWN's death. In addition,
BROWN & GREEN shall pay to BROWN's named beneficiary or in the absence of a named beneficiary,

BROWN's estate, a death benefit of $5,000, which is intended to qualify as a tax-exempt death benefit under Section 101(b) of the Internal Revenue Code or any amendments thereto.

Fifth: Expenses: GREEN & BROWN agree to reimburse BROWN for expenses incurred in connection with the conduct of the Practice including but not limited to professional license fees, dues in professional associations, subscriptions to professional journals, cost of attending professional conventions and professional meetings, entertainment expenses where the entertainment is designed to promote the Practice, and a home telephone for use in connection with the Practice.

BROWN agrees to submit necessary receipts and other documentation to support the above expenses in form sufficient to substantiate the deductibility of the expenses for income tax purposes.

Sixth: Automobile Expense: GREEN & BROWN agree to provide BROWN with an automobile and pay the cost of licensing, insuring, repairing and operating of said automobile.

Seven: Vacation: Each year during the term of this Agreement BROWN shall be entitled to a vacation and additional leave to attend conventions and professional meetings. Vacations and other leaves are subject to approval by the Board of Directors of the corporation. BROWN agrees to give reasonable prior notice of his intent to take a vacation or additional leave to attend a professional convention in order that his vacations and other leaves do not interfere with the proper operation of the corporation's business.

Eighth: Sick Leave: If BROWN becomes either physically or mentally disabled during the term of this Agreement so as not to be able to perform his full regular duties in the Practice, he is to receive his regular salary as follows:

First Six Months	75%
Next Three Months	50%
Next Three Months	25%
Thereafter	0%

The salary as determined for purposes of this Paragraph is to be reduced by the amount of any disability benefits provided for him pursuant to Paragraph Four herein.

Any disability occurring less than three months following a prior disability shall be treated as a continuation of the prior disability rather than a new disability.

Ninth: Partial Sick Leave: In the event BROWN returns to active duties in the Practice following a disability but is unable or not willing to devote his full time to the Practice, he shall receive a salary proportionate to the ratio that his reduced schedule bears to his full time regular duties.

Tenth: Two or More Disabled Professionals: If two or more licensed professional employees are disabled at the same time and the board of directors of BROWN & GREEN determine that it is unable to maintain the disability payments provided for the disabled professional employees out of current income after all disbursements other than disability compensation, then the disability payments to the professional employees including BROWN shall be reduced proportionately to such amounts as the employer is then able to pay.

Eleventh: Liability Insurance: The professional corporation shall provide professional liability or malpractice insurance with a minimum of $1,000,000 in coverage for the benefit of the corporation and BROWN. In the event the corporation fails to or is unable to provide professional liability insurance coverage in the stated amount, BROWN may procure said insurance. The corporation will reimburse BROWN for the cost of insurance obtained individually.

Twelfth: Office Expenses: The professional corporation shall provide and pay for suitable office space and facilities, including furniture, fixtures, supplies, utilities and other expenses agreed to by the board of directors of the corporation. The corporation will also provide necessary secretarial and clerical personnel.

(Editor's Note: In a medical professional corporation, provision should be made for nurses, etc.)

Thirteenth: Regulations: BROWN agrees that at all times he will observe and conform to all the laws and customs of the profession. In addition, he will at all times during the term of this Agreement comply with the reasonable directions of the board of directors of the professional corporation.

Fourteenth: Accounting: The professional corporation shall establish and maintain procedures for billing patients (clients). BROWN agrees to provide an accounting of his professional visits and monies received by him on account of the Practice. All monies received by BROWN on behalf of the Practice shall be paid over to the professional corporation to be deposited in the corporation's accounts.

Fifteenth: Property: All records concerning the Practice are the property of the professional corporation. Upon termination of this Agreement BROWN shall not be entitled to any files or records.

(Editor's Note: Files and records may be subject to the discretion of the patient or client. In many states, a patient can direct that his charts and records be transferred to another physician. Similarly, a client can direct that his file be turned over to another attorney provided, of course, that the original attorney does not have a charging lien on the file.)

Sixteenth: Management of the Practice: The responsibility for management of the Practice rests with the board of directors of the corporation. It is understood that the board of directors shall establish the professional standards to be observed, the fees to be charged, and the office hours to be maintained. BROWN shall not be required to perform any act which is a violation of the rules of the profession. BROWN agrees that in dealing with clients or prospective clients of the corporation that he will give no assurance in any form to such persons that he or any particular employee of the corporation will perform services for such client, it being understood that the board of directors of the corporation, or its designate, shall have the sole authority to determine which employees of the corporation shall perform services for any particular client of the corporation.

(Editor's Note: At this point, reference to specific rules would be helpful; e.g., in the case of a law firm, reference to the Canons of Ethics would be appropriate.)

Seventeenth: Termination: This Agreement shall terminate on the occurrence of any of the following events:

(A) Written termination agreement signed by the professional corporation and BROWN;

(B) Upon BROWN's election to retire. BROWN may retire at any time after reaching the age of 65. BROWN must retire upon reaching the age of 70. BROWN may retire with the consent of the board of directors upon reaching the age of 60;

(C) Upon BROWN's loss of his license to practice;

(D) Upon BROWN's death;

(E) Upon BROWN's giving ninety days' notice to the professional corporation of his intention to terminate this agreement. BROWN shall not give notice of his intent to terminate the Agreement during any period in which any other licensed professional who is a shareholder in the professional corporation is disabled and collecting disability or sick pay pursuant to the provisions of Paragraph Eighth of this Agreement;

(F) Upon the corporation giving ninety days' notice to BROWN. The corporation may not terminate this Agreement by giving notice while BROWN is receiving disability pay pursuant to Paragraph Fourth of this Agreement;

(G) Upon BROWN becoming permanently and totally disabled so that he is unable to satisfactorily perform his regular full time duties. If BROWN is disabled for twelve consecutive months, he shall be considered permanently and totally disabled pursuant to the terms of this Paragraph.

Eighteenth: Arbitration: Any disputes arising under this Agreement are to be settled by arbitration under the rules of the American Arbitration Association. The award of the arbitrator or arbitrators appointed in accordance with the rules of the American Arbitration Association shall be binding upon the parties hereto, and judgment on the award may be entered by any court having competent jurisdiction.

Nineteenth: Amendments: This Agreement may not be modified, amended, added to, or changed except by a writing signed by both the professional corporation and BROWN. The Agreement may be terminated in accordance with the terms of Paragraph Seventeenth of this Agreement.

Twentieth: Parties: This Agreement shall be binding upon the parties, their legal representatives, successors and assigns.

Twenty-First: Notices: All notices provided for herein shall be in writing and served upon the parties at the following addresses unless the addresses for service of such notices have been changed by the parties.

PROFESSIONAL CORPORATION

_____

_____

_____

BROWN

_____

_____

All notices served pursuant to this Agreement shall be served by personal service or certified mail, return receipt requested.

Twenty-Second: Governing Law: This Agreement shall be governed by the laws of the State of _____.

IN WITNESS WHEREOF THE PARTIES HAVE SET THEIR HANDS AND SEALS THE _____ day of _____, 19_____.

_____

BROWN

_____

BROWN & GREEN

SPECIMEN FORMS FOR SHAREHOLDER AGREEMENTS

The forms set out below have been developed to provide for transition and redemption in the event a shareholder dies or withdraws. The form set out at 911.1 provides that valuation is to be based on a formula. The form set out at 911.2 utilizes an annual agreement between shareholders.

911.1 Shareholders' Agreement—Valuation Based on a Formula

AGREEMENT made this the _____ day of _____ 19_____ by and between (insert names of shareholders) hereinafter sometimes referred to as the shareholders, and (insert name of the professional corporation) hereinafter sometimes referred to as the professional corporation.

WHEREAS the parties are desirous of providing for the orderly continuation of the affairs of the corporation in the event of the death, incapacity, disqualification or termination of employment of any of the shareholders of the corporation, and

WHEREAS the parties are desirous of providing for the purchase of the shares of shareholders who die, become incapacitated, or disqualified from the practice (insert profession).

WHEREAS the parties are all members of the _____ profession and recognize that under the applicable law all shareholders of the corporation must be members of the _____profession.

NOW THEREFORE BE IT AGREED BETWEEN THE PARTIES

First: Purchase of Shares: The professional corporation agrees that it will redeem the shares held by any shareholder or the estate of any shareholder, or instead will facilitate a purchase of said shares by the other shareholders, pursuant to Paragraph Second, upon any of the following events:

    (a) The death of a shareholder;

    (b) The disqualification of a shareholder to practice _____ _____;

    (c) The disability of a shareholder to continue to practice _____ _____;

    (d) The termination of the shareholder's agreement with the professional corporation pursuant to the provisions of the employment agreement dated _____ _____.

Second: Purchase by Other Shareholders: In the event the corporation elects not to purchase the shares held by a shareholder whose shares are to be redeemed pursuant to Paragraph First of this agreement, the remaining shareholders may purchase the shares in proportion to their holding of stock in the corporation. Sales to the individual shareholder must be approved by a majority of the shareholders remaining after the withdrawal or death of the shareholder whose shares are being redeemed. In the event the shareholders decide to purchase the shares held by a departing shareholder individually and any shareholder is unwilling or unable to purchase his share of the shares owned by the departing shareholder, the corporation will purchase the shares.

For the purpose of this Paragraph the term disqualification shall be defined as meaning the permanent loss of the right to practice (insert profession) or the acceptance by the shareholder, without permission of a majority of the other shareholders, of employment which substantially impairs the shareholder's legal right to practice (insert profession) or substantially reduces the time which the shareholder may devote to the professional corporation's practice.

For the purpose of this Paragraph Second, the term "personal disability or incapacity" means a physical or mental condition which prevents the shareholder from practicing his profession for more than twenty hours per week for a period of twenty weeks.

Third: Transfers to Third Parties: The shareholders may transfer their interest in the professional corporation only upon the approval of the stockholders holding a majority of the outstanding shares of the corporation. For purposes of approving the transfer of stock the stock to be transferred cannot be voted. If the shareholders of the corporation refuse to authorize the transfer to a third party, they agree to purchase such shares in proportion to their ownership in the professional corporation for the price determined in accordance with Paragraph Fifth of this agreement or the bona fide good faith price offered by the proposed third party purchaser, whichever is less.

Fourth: Dissolution: Notwithstanding the provision of this agreement, if a shareholder seeks to sell his shares of stock in the corporation to a third party not approved by the other shareholders, a majority of the remaining shareholders may vote to dissolve the corporation.

Fifth: Determination of Redemption Price: The purchase price of the shares to be purchased by the corporation or the other shareholders in accordance with the terms of this agreement is to be determined by the corporation's regular accountants by converting the professional corporation's cash basis balance sheet into an accrual balance sheet using regularly accepted accounting practices. In converting the cash balance sheet into the accrual balance sheet, a reserve of ten per cent is to be established for all accounts receivables and work in progress. The accounts payable, unearned income, prepaid expenses and income taxes are to be accrued. The accrual basis balance sheet is to be adjusted in accordance with the following formula:

Five per cent is to be subtracted from net accounts receivable and work in progress;

The value of any life insurance on the life of a deceased shareholder is to be excluded;

The book value of any real property is to be increased or decreased to fair market value.

In the event the shareholder or his estate cannot agree, the fair market value of the property shall be determined by the average of three appraisals, one made by an appraiser selected by the corporation, one by an appraiser selected by the departing shareholder or the estate of a deceased shareholder, and the third selected by the two original appraisers. The appraisers are to determine the "fair market value" of the property. The cost of the appraisal is to be divided evenly between the corporation and the departing shareholder or the estate of the deceased shareholder.

The value of the shares is to be the book value of the shares as determined from the balance sheet adjusted as indicated above.

Sixth: Payment: The purchase price for the shares to be redeemed is to be paid to the shareholder or his estate in cash in accordance with the following schedule:

Within six months of the disability or the appointment of an administrator or executor of decedent's estate provided the redemption is occurring because of the shareholder's death of disability;

Within sixty days of the failure of the remaining shareholders to approve the transfer of shares in the professional corporation to another professional;

Within sixty days of the purchase or redemption of the shares.

Seventh: Note as Payment: Either the professional corporation or the remaining shareholders may pay for the purchase of the shares of stock in the corporation by delivering a promissory note to the shareholder or his estate within the time limits for making cash payments as specified in this agreement. The note is to bear interest at the rate of 7.5 per cent per annum and shall provide the debtor with the privilege of prepaying at any time. If the promissory note is made by the professional corporation, it must be personally guaranteed by the shareholders remaining in the practice.

Eighth: Restriction on Share Certificates: All shares of stock in the professional corporation shall bear the following restrictive notice.

NOTICE: These shares may not be sold, mortgaged, hypothecated or transferred except in accordance with the provision of a certain agreement dated _____, a copy of which is available for inspection at the offices of the corporation during normal business hours.

Ninth: Additional Shareholders: The parties agree that all new shareholders will be required to sign a counterpart of this agreement prior to the issuance of shares in the corporation.

Tenth: Termination: This agreement may be amended or terminated only upon the agreement of all of the shareholders of the corporation which agreement must be in writing. The agreement will automatically terminate upon the dissolution or bankruptcy of the corporation or if there is only one remaining shareholder of the corporation.

Eleventh: Default by Corporation: In the event the professional corporation is unable to make the purchase required by this agreement as a result of any financial limitation imposed by statute, loan arrangements, or any other legal reason, the shareholders agree to take such steps and cause the corporation to take such steps as may be necessary to enable the corporation to purchase the shares. In the event it is not possible to take such steps, the parties agree that the individual shareholders will purchase the shares in the corporation which would otherwise have been purchased by the professional corporation, such shares to be purchased in proportion to the shareholders' stock in the professional corporation.

Twelfth: Governing Law: The parties agree that this agreement shall be governed in accordance with the laws of the State of _____.

Thirteenth: Binding Effect: The parties agree that this agreement shall be binding upon them, their successors and assigns including personal representatives, executors, administrators, heirs and legatees.

IN WITNESS WHEREOF the parties have set their hands and seals on the first day above written.

911.2 Shareholders' Agreement—Valuation Based on Yearly Agreement Among Shareholders

AGREEMENT made this _____ day of _____,
19_____ by and between JOHN JONES, M.D., a licensed physician residing at 122 Main Street, New York, New York; ROBERT BROWN, M.D., a licensed physician residing at 122 East Street, New York, New York; and JAMES GREEN, M.D., a licensed physician residing at 122 West Street, New York, New York, all of whom are hereafter sometimes referred to as SHAREHOLDERS; and JONES, BROWN AND GREEN PROFESSIONAL CORPORATION, a professional corporation incorporated under and by virtue of the laws of the State of New York, having its office at 222 Main Street, New York, New York, hereinafter sometimes known as CORPORATION.

WHEREAS the parties are desirous to enter into an agreement providing for the orderly transfer of the corporation's funds in the event of the death, retirement, disability or withdrawal of any of the shareholders of the corporation;

WHEREAS the parties are desirous of providing for the admission of new shareholders to the corporation.

NOW BE IT AGREED THAT:

First: Election of Directors: Each shareholder agrees to vote his stock in the corporation so as to elect the following directors:

> JOHN JONES
> ROBERT BROWN
> JAMES GREEN

Second: Election of Officers: The parties agree that the Corporation's Certificate of Incorporation and Bylaws are to provide for the election of officers by the shareholders in accordance with the provisions of the New York Business Corporation Law. SHAREHOLDERS agree to cause the election of the following officers:

> JOHN JONES   President
> ROBERT BROWN   Vice-President & Secretary
> JAMES GREEN   Treasurer

Third: Compensation: The salaries and other benefits paid to each of the officers of the corporation shall be equal. The difference if any between the salaries, fringe benefits and other items of compensation shall be equalized by the payment of bonuses as an added item of deferred compensation, or such other method of payment or reimbursement as each employee shall elect in writing.

Fourth: Shareholder Status: In the event any employee ceases to be a shareholder of the professional corporation his office as a director and as an officer shall be automatically declared vacant. This agreement constitutes each shareholder's resignation as an officer and as a director of Corporation in the event he ceases to be a shareholder of Corporation. This paragraph does not affect the terms of any employment agreement between Corporation and the Employees.

Fifth: Disposition of Compensation in Event of Withdrawal: Any salary, fringe benefits, deferred compensation or other benefits which any party forfeits because of the terms of any employment agreement, consultation or deferred compensation arrangements shall inure to the benefit of the remaining employee-shareholders in compensation for the increased services which they shall be required to perform as a result of the withdrawal or retirement of an employee-shareholder. Their share of forfeited amounts shall be paid to the employees currently as additional bonus compensation or subsequently as an item of deferred compensation or any other method as shall be elected by the employee.

Sixth: Shares Subject to Agreement: The shareholders agree that all shares of stock in the professional corporation issued to them or others are subject to the terms of this agreement and that a statement to that effect in accordance with the language of Paragraph Nineteenth shall be printed on the share certificates. No additional shares shall be issued unless, prior to the issuance of the new shares, the new shareholders agree to be bound by the terms of this agreement as if they were original parties hereto.

Seventh: Restrictions on Stock Transfer: The parties recognize that under New York law, unless otherwise agreed to between them, upon the death or disqualification of a shareholder within six months after the appointment of the executor or administrator of his estate, or within six months after his disqualification, the corporation is required to purchase or redeem his shares at book value as of the end of the month immediately preceding the death or disqualification. The parties wish to make other provision regarding the transfer and succession of a shareholder's shares of stock in the corporation. It is agreed that the provision of New York's Professional Corporation Law referred to above shall not be applicable to this Corporation and its Shareholders and that instead the procedure set forth in Paragraphs Eighth and Ninth shall apply.

Eighth: Transfer of Shares: No shareholder without the express written consent of the other shareholders shall sell, assign, mortgage, hypothecate, transfer, pledge or vote a security interest, encumber or otherwise dispose of any of his shares of stock in the Corporation now owned or hereafter acquired during the term of this agreement in any manner other than as permitted by this agreement.

Ninth: Shares Transferred in Violation of Agreement: No sale, assignment, mortgage, hypothecation, transfer, pledge, security interest, lien, encumbrance, gift or other disposition of any of the shares of this corporation by any shareholder in violation of the provisions of this agreement, the Certificate of Incorporation and the Bylaws shall be valid and the corporation shall not transfer any shares on the books of the corporation nor shall any shares be entitled to vote, nor shall any dividends be paid on any shares during the period of any violation of this agreement. The provisions of this Paragraph shall be in addition to and not in lieu of any other remedies legal or equitable to enforce the provisions of this agreement. Further, the parties expressly waive any voting dividend or appraisal rights which would otherwise be entitled except as provided for in this agreement.

Tenth: Redemption on Disability, Retirement and Death: In the event a shareholder retires, becomes disabled, or dies, Corporation shall within 180 days of the shareholder's death, retirement or his becoming disabled redeem his stock. The redemption price shall be the amount set forth in the certificate of valuation. (Exhibit A) attached to and made a part of this agreement.

Eleventh: Certificate of Valuation: Each year on or before the 31st day of December, the shareholders shall endorse the agreed valuation amount to be used for the succeeding year.

Twelfth: Alternative Valuation: In the event the parties fail to agree upon a valuation amount as required by Paragraph Eleventh of this agreement and a death occurs, a shareholder becomes disabled or retires, the redemption price shall be the greater of the amount as fixed by the last certificate of valuation agreed to by the shareholders, or the book value of the shares as set forth on the books and records of the corporation, adjusted, however, to eliminate all accounts receivable and to substitute the fair market value of stocks, bonds, mortgages, real estate or other types of investments instead of the book value of those items.

Thirteenth: Payment of Redemption Price: The redemption price for a shareholder's shares as provided for herein shall be paid in a lump sum in cash at the closing of the sale.

Fourteenth: Restrictions on Redemption: In the event the corporation is prohibited from redeeming the shares because of financial limitations or restrictions, the remaining shareholders shall purchase the stock of the retiring, withdrawing, deceased or disabled shareholder on the same terms and conditions as set forth for redemption.

Fifteenth: Voluntary Redemption: A shareholder seeking to have his stock redeemed other than because of retirement, death or disability must notify the professional corporation and other shareholders in writing of his intention to do so and as soon as practicable, but not later than 90 days after receipt of the notice, the corporation shall redeem, or the remaining shareholders shall purchase, the terminating shareholder's shares of stock of the corporation for the purchase price payable in the manner herein provided for a redemption.

Sixteenth: Expulsion: The other shareholders of the professional corporation may expel a shareholder upon any of the following occurrences:

(1) A shareholder loses his license to practice.

(2) A shareholder engages in personal misconduct or breaches the employment agreement or this agreement provided the violation makes his continued presence as a shareholder in the professional corporation personally or professionally obnoxious or detrimental to the other shareholders of the professional corporation.

(3) A shareholder is expelled or otherwise disciplined by a final action of any professional or scientific organization on serious grounds other than for nonpayment of dues or similar grounds.

(4) A shareholder resigns from any professional or scientific organization under threat of disciplinary action, on serious grounds other than for nonpayment of dues or other similar grounds.

(5) A shareholder is convicted of a felony or crime involving a breach of medical ethics, moral turpitude or immoral conduct.

(6) A shareholder becomes insolvent, makes an assignment for the benefit of creditors, is declared bankrupt or his assets are administered in any type of creditor proceedings.

Seventeenth: Procedure for Expulsion: A shareholder can be expelled only by a majority vote of the shares outstanding. No shareholder may be expelled without at least 20 days' prior written notice, which notice shall state the reason for the expulsion and shall be signed by the shareholders owning a majority of the outstanding shares of stock of the corporation. The notice of expulsion required by this Paragraph must be delivered personally to the shareholder or mailed, certified mail, return receipt requested. Upon the delivery of the notice, the recipient's rights as a shareholder are to cease and his shares of stock in the corporation are to be redeemed effective as of the date fixed in the notice.

Upon expulsion, the professional corporation must pay to the expelled shareholder the purchase price provided herein for redemptions. The payment must be made as soon as practicable, but within 90 days following the service of the notice of expulsion required by this Paragraph.

Eighteenth: Transfer of Stock: In the event stock is redeemed by the estate of a deceased shareholder or by a shareholder who has retired, been expelled, or has become disabled, the shareholder agrees for himself and his estate to endorse and deliver the stock to the corporation upon receipt of the payment in redemption.

Nineteenth: Endorsement on Stock Certificate: The certificates for the stock of the corporation held by the shareholders and all other certificates for shares of stock issued after the effective date of this agreement are to be endorsed with the following legend:

NOTICE: The sale, assignment, mortgage, hypothecation, transfer, pledge, security, interest, lien, encumbrance, gift or other disposition of this stock is subject to an agreement between this corporation and its shareholders dated _____.

Twentieth: Termination: This agreement may be terminated upon the occurrence of any of the following events:

The agreement of all of the parties;

The bankruptcy or insolvency of any party to the action prior to the purchase of any stock under the terms of this agreement;

The dissolution or liquidation of the corporation prior to the purchase of any stock under the agreement.

Twenty-First: Dissolution: Each shareholder agrees to vote all of his shares of stock in the corporation for the dissolution of the corporation upon the demand of any party or upon the occurrence of any of the following events:

(1) The decision of an arbitrator or arbitrators designated to resolve any disputes between the parties to this agreement that the professional corporation is to be dissolved.

(2) Upon the written request of the holders of two-thirds of the shares of stock in the professional corporation. The written request provided for under this Paragraph must be delivered to each shareholder.

(3) The death of any shareholder if the shares of the corporation held by that stockholder are not redeemed pursuant to the provisions of this Paragraph.

Twenty-Second: Arbitration: The parties agree that any disputes between them are to be decided by arbitration under the rules of the American Arbitration Association. The arbitration is to be carried out in New York City. The award of an arbitrator or arbitrators shall be final and binding and judgment on the award may be entered by any court having competent jurisdiction.

Twenty-Third: Amendments: This agreement may be amended only by a writing signed by all of the parties. No modification, amendment additional to, or termination of this agreement which is not in writing shall be binding upon the parties hereto.

Twenty-Fourth: Binding Effect: This agreement is binding on the parties hereto, their distributees, legal representatives, successors and assigns.

Twenty-Fifth: Notices: All notices under this agreement shall be in writing and shall be served by personal service or by certified mail, return receipt requested. Notice by mail shall be addressed to the parties at the following address:

John Jones	122 Main Street, N.Y., N.Y.
Robert Brown	122 East Street, N.Y., N.Y.
James Green	122 West Street, N.Y., N.Y.
Jones, Brown & Green	222 Main Street, N.Y., N.Y.

The address for receipt of notices under this agreement may be changed by notifying each of the parties in writing of the intent to change the address for mailing notices.

Twenty-Sixth: Governing Law: This agreement shall be governed in accordance with the laws of the State of New York.

IN WITNESS WHEREOF the parties have set their hands and seals on the first day above written.

Model Medical
Reimbursement Plan

UNANIMOUS ACTION OF DIRECTORS
OF

_____

     We the undersigned being all directors of _____,
pursuant to the provisions of _____,
hereby take the following actions with the same effect as if taken at a duly called meeting of the directors.

     WHEREAS, counsel for the corporation has advised that the   *Employee Welfare*
employee welfare plans maintained by the corporation must contain certain   *Plans–ERISA*
additional provisions concerning fiduciary responsibility and setting forth **a**   *Provisions*
claims procedure in order that the plans will comply with the Employee Retirement Income Security Act
of 1974 (ERISA), and the corporation desires to amend all of its welfare plans to incorporate these
provisions, the amendment to be effective as of January 1, 1975, the effective date specified by ERISA,

     THEREFORE, BE IT RESOLVED, that the corporation hereby amends its employee
welfare plans to add the following provisions, this amendment to be effective as of January 1, 1975:

     1. The President of the corporation is   *Named*
hereby designated as the "named fiduciary" for each of the   *Fiduciary*
welfare plans maintained by the corporation for its employees, and he shall have the
authority to control and manage the operation and administration of such plans.
Provided, however, that in the case of a corporate welfare plan under which the benefits
are provided in whole or in part by an insurance policy, the company that issued the
policy shall be the "named fiduciary" of that plan with regard to the review and final
decisions on a claim for the benefits under its policy, instead of the President, as
provided in the Claims Procedure for the corporation's welfare plans set forth below.

     2. The President may allocate his respon-   *Allocation of*
sibilities for the operation and administration of any corpo-   *Fiduciary*
rate welfare plan, including the designation of persons who   *Responsibilities*
are not named fiduciaries to carry out fiduciary responsibilities under any such plan.
The President shall effect such allocation of his responsibilities by delivering to the
corporation a written instrument signed by him that specifies the nature and extent of
the responsibilities allocated, including, if appropriate, the persons, not named
fiduciaries, who are designated to carry out fiduciary responsibilities under the particular plan or plans.

     3. By resolution duly adopted, the Board   *Amendment*
of Directors may at any time amend or terminate any of the   *Procedure*
corporation's welfare plans.

     4. Payments shall be made to and from   *Basis of*
each of the corporation's welfare plans in the manner pro-   *Payment*
vided in the particular plan.

     5. The following claims procedure shall   *Claims*
apply to each of the corporation's welfare plans: *Procedure*

     a. *Filing of a Claim for Benefits.* A participant or beneficiary of
any corporate welfare plan shall make a claim for the benefits provided under **a**
particular plan in the manner provided in that plan.

b. *Notification to Claimant of Decision.* If a claim is wholly or partially denied, notice of the decisions, meeting the requirement of paragraph c following, shall be furnished to the claimant within a reasonable period of time after receipt of the claim by the plan.

c. *Content of Notice.* The corporation, or the designated plan administrator if a plan administrator other than the corporation has been designated for a particular plan, shall provide to every claimant who is denied a claim for benefits written notice setting forth in a manner calculated to be understood by the claimant, the following:

(1) The specific reason or reasons for the denial;

(2) Specific reference to pertinent plan provisions on which the denial is based;

(3) A description of any additional material or information necessary for the claimant to perfect the claim and an explanation of why such material or information is necessary; and

(4) An explanation of the plan's claim review procedure, as set forth in paragraphs d, e, and f following:

d. *Review Procedure.* The purpose of the review procedure set forth in this paragraph and in paragraphs e and f following is to provide a procedure by which a claimant under each of the corporation's welfare plans may have a reasonable opportunity to appeal a denial of a claim to an appropriate named fiduciary for a full and fair review. To accomplish that purpose, the claimant or his duly authorized representative:

(1) May request a review upon written application to the particular plan involved.

(2) May review pertinent plan documents; and

(3) May submit issues and comments in writing.

A claimant (or his duly authorized representative) shall request a review by filing a written application for review with the plan at any time within sixty (60) days after receipt by the claimant of written notice of the denial of his claim.

e. *Decisions on Review.* A decision on review of a denied claim shall be made in the following manner:

(1) The decision on review shall be made by the President, who may in his discretion hold a hearing on the denied claim. The President shall make his decisions promptly, and not later than sixty (60) days after the plan's receipt of the request for review, unless special circumstances (such as the need to hold a hearing) require an extension of time for processing, in which case a decision shall be rendered as soon as possible, but not later than one hundred twenty (120) days after receipt of the request for review.

(2) The decision on review shall be in writing and shall include specific reasons for the decisions, written in a manner calculated to be understood by the claimant, and specific references to the pertinent plan provisions on which the decision is based.

f. *Claims Procedure for an Insured Welfare Plan.* In the case of a corporate welfare plan under which the benefits are provided in whole or in part under a policy issued by an insurance company, the review and final decisions on a claim for benefits under the policy shall be made by the insurance company that issued the policy. With respect to a claim for benefits under an insurance policy, the company that issued the policy shall be the entity which reviews and makes decisions on claim denials, and it shall be the "named fiduciary" of that particular plan with regard to review and final decision on a claim for benefits under its policy, instead of the President.

———————————————————————

President

UNANIMOUS ACTION OF DIRECTORS
OF

_____

We the undersigned, being all the directors of _____,
pursuant to the provisions of _____,
hereby take the following actions with the same effect as if taken at a duly called meeting of the directors.

WHEREAS, the Board of Directors of the corporation considers it desirable and in the best interests of the corporation that it provide a plan for the reimbursement by the corporation of medical expenses incurred by its full-time officers for themselves, their spouses, and dependents, which expenses are not otherwise reimbursed under policies of medical insurance, in order to provide encouragement to the officers and further secure their association with the corporation as employees on a long-term basis, and

WHEREAS, in the judgement of the Board of Directors, the full-time officers of the corporation all perform significant executive and managerial services, and they form a distinct class of employees, each of whose services are similar to each other and dissimilar to the services rendered by other employees, and it is the desire of the Board to limit this Plan to the corporation's executive and managerial employees, all of whom are included in the classification of "full-time officers," and

WHEREAS, it is the intention of the Board of Directors to include other employees in the Plan at such future time as they render executive and managerial services comparable to those now performed by the employees covered by the Plan,

THEREFORE, BE IT RESOLVED, that the corporation hereby adopts a Medical Expense Reimbursement Plan covering the full-time officers of the corporation, as follows:

A.   The corporation shall reimburse each of its full-time officers for all medical expenses to the extent provided in this resolution. For purposes of this resolution, medical expenses of employees shall include physicians', surgeons' and dentists' fees, hospital charges (including laboratory and x-ray fees), costs of medical related aids such as eye glasses, and costs of medical and hospitalization insurance, major medical insurance and disability insurance (including the costs of any group insurance plans which the corporation may adopt). Medical expenses of an employee shall include those incurred with respect to the employee himself, a spouse of an employee, and any dependent children of an employee. There shall be no reimbursement to the extent there is other reimbursement such as through insurance, damages, or otherwise.

B.   "Officer" shall mean an officer or assistant officer of the corporation. "Full-time Officer" shall mean an officer whose customary employment is 1,000 hours or more in a calendar year.

C.   "Medical Expenses" shall mean those costs for medical and dental care defined under Section 213(e) of the Internal Revenue Code of 1954. "Dependents" shall mean those persons defined as dependents under section 152 of the Internal Revenue Code.

D.   The maximum amount of medical expense reimbursement for any employee in any calendar year shall not exceed 10% of the employee's annual cash compensation.

In order to comply with the provisions of Sections 102 and 503 of the Employee Retirement Income Security Act of 1974, the following provisions are also deemed to be part of this plan:

(a)   The plan will be administered by the Board of Directors of the corporation and the President of the corporation is hereby designated as agent for the plan for the service of legal process.

(b)   In addition to any eligibility requirements stated above, a participant or his beneficiary in the plan may be retroactively disqualified from receiving any benefits from the corporation pursuant to the plan if the Board of Directors determine that the participant has been guilty of an act of dishonesty, destruction of company property or unauthorized disclosure of confidential business information of the corporation. Also, the Board shall have the right to retroactively change or cancel the plan at any time for any reason whatsoever, except as otherwise noted above.

(c)   All benefits which result from the provisions of this plan will be paid from the general assets of the corporation. No director or officer of the corporation shall be personally liable for any benefits due a participant or his beneficiary pursuant to this plan.

(d)   The plan is administered and plan records are maintained on a calendar basis.

(e)   A participant or his beneficiary shall present in writing all claims for benefits under the plan to the directors. The directors shall respond to any such claim within three months in writing or orally, as the case may be.

(f)   To receive reimbursement under the Plan, an officer shall submit suitable written proof of expenses to the corporation. Questions as to whether an expense is reimbursable under the Plan shall be resolved in accordance with the corporation's Claims Procedure for its welfare plans.

(g)   The Board shall provide adequate notice in writing to any participant or beneficiary whose claim for benefits has been denied and shall be afforded a reasonable opportunity to have a full and fair review by the Board of their decision denying the claim.

This plan is intended to comply with the provisions of Parts 1, 3 and 5 of the Employee Retirement Income Security Act of 1974, and, therefore, will be deemed to be automatically amended to comply with all appropriate regulations to these parts, issued by any appropriate government agency as of the effective date of each such regulation.

The above actions are effective _____, 19_____.

_____
President

Bibliography

Burke, William J. and Zaloom, Basil J., *BLUEPRINT FOR PROFESSIONAL SERVICE COR-
PORATIONS*, Dun & Bradstreet, Inc., with Thomas J. Crowell Co., New York
(1970)

Lasser, S. Jay, *EVERYONE'S 1976 INCOME TAX GUIDE*, Pyramid Publications Div. of Pyramid
Communications, Inc., 919 Third Avenue, New York, New York 10022 (1975)

Nicholas, Ted. *HOW TO FORM YOUR OWN CORPORATION WITHOUT A LAWYER FOR
UNDER $50*, Enterprise Publishing Co., Beneficial Building, 1300 Market Street,
Wilmington, DE 19801 (1974)

PROFESSIONAL CORPORATION DESK BOOK, Institute for Business Planning, Inc., IBP Plaza,
Englewood Cliffs, New Jersey 07632 (1975)

Siegel, Edward. *DEFEND YOURSELF!*, Fawcett World Library (1973)

Stoeber, Edward A., *TAX AND FRINGE BENEFIT PLANNING FOR PROFESSIONAL COR-
PORATIONS*, The National Underwriter Company, 420 East Fourth Street, Cincin-
nati, Ohio 45202

Periodicals
THE FINANCIAL PLANNER, Environs Publishing Company, 6201 W. Cermak Road, Berwyn,
Illinois 60402 (September 1975)

MEDICAL ECONOMICS, Medical Economics Company, Division of Litton Industries, Oradell, New
Jersey 07649 (March 8, 22, April 5, 1976)

MONEY, Time, Inc., 541 North Fairbanks Court, Chicago, Illinois 60611 (April, June, 1976)

PHYSICIAN'S MANAGEMENT, Harcourt Brace Jovanovich, Health Care Publications, 4015 W.
65th St., Minneapolis, Minn. 55435 (April 1976)

WALL STREET JOURNAL, Dow Jones, Inc., 22 Cortlandt St., New York, N.Y. 10007 (1976)

Glossary

ACCRUAL-BASIS ACCOUNTING
Keeping books and paying taxes on a basis of when costs are incurred, rather than when paid.

ALIEN CORPORATION
One licensed to operate in a state although it is incorporated in another state.

ANCILLARY ACTIVITIES
Those related to the corporation and the profession but usually parallel, tangential, or irregular in nature.

ANNUITY
Periodic payment, usually annual, from any capital source; associated with retirement plans.

ARBITRATION
The submission of a dispute between corporation members to an agreed-to referee.

ARTICLES OF INCORPORATION
Required basic document establishing principal facts and features of a corporation, its founders, director and owners.

BYLAWS
Policies established in writing by shareholders or directors for governing the operations of a corporation.

C. P. A.
Certified Public Accountant; a licensed professional accountant.

CAPITAL ASSETS
Tangible assets of a company, such as owned real estate, equipment, furnishings, vehicles, etc.

CAPITAL GAINS
The appreciation in dollar value of properties, including intangibles. Short-term is ownership turnover in less than nine months, or less than 12 months, effective 1978 with resulting full taxation; long-term gains are taxed at half the short-term rate.

CASH-BASIS ACCOUNTING
Keeping books and paying taxes on a basis of when costs are paid, rather than when incurred.

CERTIFICATE, STOCK
Document showing a quantity of shares in a corporation, the owner of the stated quantity, and information covering rights and limitations of ownership, including class of stock, par value, if any, whether voting stock, etc.

CERTIFICATE OF INCORPORATION
Document issued by a state, usually the secretary of state, authorizing a corporation to conduct business in that state.

DOMESTIC CORPORATION
One chartered in the same state in which it conducts business.

CERTIFICATE OF LICENSE
Document issued by a state regulating board acknowledging the licensed status of a professional person.

CLOSE CORPORATION
A corporation owned by one person or a small group of persons known to each other, and the ownership shares are not for public sale.

COLLAPSIBLE CORPORATION
A term applied by the IRS to a company whose assets are almost entirely the product of its members' individual service, with the so-called corporation contributing virtually nothing otherwise. Attempt by IRS at liquidation or owner-

ship transfer to shift corporate assets to owners for taxation as personal income.

COMMON STOCK

The market value of a corporation expressed in shares of fluctuating value; invariably the majority if not the only class of stock, receiving whatever dividends the directors decide; the only stock with voting rights.

CORPORATION

A form of organization gaining increasing favor in business and the professions because it provides virtually all the benefits available to an individual, plus other benefits not otherwise available, especially in tax reductions and net gains.

CUMULATIVE VOTING RIGHTS

A shareholder's right to vote all his shares to a single director, his total multiplied by the number of nominees; protects minority representation.

DEFERRED SALARY

Part of one's salary shifted from high-income, high-tax years to lower-income, lower-tax years, usually during retirement.

DIRECTOR

Basic policymaker of a corporation, elected by shareholders for a specified period of time. May or may not be a shareholder or employee.

DIVIDEND

Portion of net (after tax) profit distributed to shareholders in addition to or instead of a bonus. Other portion reinvested in capital improvements or left to accumulate.

ERISA

Employee Retirement Income Security Act signed into law in 1974 to provide minimum national standards and benefits in plans providing retirement income.

EXECUTIVE COMMITTEE

A committee consisting of directors and officers and setting day-to-day policy for a corporation within the basic policy framework. Usually a feature only of large corporations.

FILING FEE

Specified fee paid to a state by the incorporators of a corporation when applying for original charter or annual renewal. Amount depends on the state and capitalization of corporation, minimums ranging from $5 to over $100.

FISCAL YEAR

Date other than January 1 fixed arbitrarily by a corporation for tax advantages based on seasonal aspect of receipts and expenditures.

FIXED-BENEFIT PENSION PLAN

A type of retirement plan providing a fixed, predictable retirement income, usually favored by older employees because absence of legal limitations on funding (though not on payout) provides more retirement income in less time than do other types of plans.

FRINGE BENEFITS

A corporation can provide its owner—employees with many benefits other than direct compensation, including cheaper insurance, full deductions for medical costs, limited business liability, lower taxes on investment income and death benefits, larger pensions, etc.

FUNDING

The method of providing capital to meet an obligation; in the context of our subject, the sources of capitalizing fringe benefits.

GROSS INCOME

The total yearly income from all sources before disbursements to meet operating costs and fixed obligations.

IRA

Individual Retirement Account; a federal act designed for workers not covered by a company pension plan.

IRC

Internal Revenue Code; the federal code covering all forms of taxation at the federal level.

IRS

Internal Revenue Service; federal bureau responsible for collecting federal revenue under a code enacted by Congress; does not have police powers, but can sue alleged violators.

INCORPORATOR

The person, or one of several persons, who organize a corporation and apply for its charter.

INDEMNIFICATION

In our context, statement in bylaws providing for reimbursement to officers and directors for personal expenses incurred for any corporate litigation.

INSURANCE PREMIUMS

The payments made by, or on behalf of, the insured to an insurance company or agency.

INTEGRATION LEVEL

In a retirement plan integrated with Social Security, the point between two levels of contribution to the plan by the corporation, the level being a choice

within formula parameters established by federal law.

KEOGH PLAN

An attempt at the federal level to provide self-employed persons with the same retirement benefits available generally to employees of companies providing them with retirement programs. Grants deferred taxation on income paid into the plan, within certain limitations.

LIQUIDATION

Turning paper assets into spendable assets; also in this book, the dissolution of a corporation and distribution of its assets.

MINUTES

The written record of each official directors' and stockholders' meeting.

MONEY-PURCHASE PLAN

A type of corporate retirement plan funded through contributions based on compensation percentage within limits set by law. Popular among younger employees since it can provide larger retirement benefits than a fixed-benefit plan when in force over a longer period of time.

NET INCOME

What is left from all income sources after operating costs and fixed obligations have been met. This is not taxable income.

OFFICER

Person given prescribed authority by directors or shareholders for day-to-day operation of the corporation. Four offices usually recognized by law are president, vice president, secretary and treasurer. They may or may not be shareholders and/or directors.

OPERATING CAPITAL

Sum of money required to meet current operating expenses of all kinds; such expenses are income tax-deductible.

ORDINARY LIFE INSURANCE

See "permanent life insurance."

PAID-IN CAPITAL

Amount of money received by a corporation in return for issued shares of stock, and representing the valuation of the corporation based on its assets.

PAR VALUE

Theoretically, the value of a corporation divided by the number of shares issued gave the par value of a share. Realistically, par value has nothing to do with market value, and today, most corporations issue no-par stock.

PARTNERSHIP

Two or more persons formally associated in a common enterprise, but not organized as a corporation.

PASSIVE INCOME

Income derived from investment of capital, and not as compensation for one's labor.

PERMANENT LIFE INSURANCE

Also called "whole life," "ordinary life," or "straight life" insurance. The investment kind of insurance that builds cash value and a future return, as opposed to term insurance that pays a specified amount only on claims.

PERSONAL HOLDING COMPANY

By IRS definition, a company having, for the last half of a taxable year, more than half the value of its stock owned by fewer than six stockholders and receiving at least 60 per cent of its income in the form of passive income and personal service contracts.

PERSONAL SERVICE CONTRACTS

Service for which the person receiving the service designates the person who will perform it.

PREEMPTIVE RIGHTS

The right of a shareholder to buy shares in proportion to the number of shares that he holds; helps control ownership of a corporation.

PREFERRED STOCK

A class of stock offering priority payment of a fixed dividend, but no voting rights. In distribution of assets it takes precedence over common stock.

PRIME LENDING RATE

The interest rate charged by banks to their highest-credit customers—usually large corporations. It invariably runs one to two percentage points below the lowest rate available on personal loans or mortgages.

PROFESSION

For purposes of incorporating a practice, it means any personal service occupation requiring certification by a state regulating board and licensing by a state. It does not include licensed trades such as plumbing and electrical contracting services.

PROFIT

The difference between income on the one hand and the total cost of earning the income on the other hand. Gross profit is gross income minus investment and overhead, or operating costs; net profit is gross profit minus taxes paid.

PROFIT-SHARING

A system of allocating profits to an investment plan on behalf of employees, usually for a retirement program.

PROPRIETORSHIP

The label in business assigned to a one-man ownership of an unincorporated enterprise.

PROXY VOTE

Voting one's shares in absentia through another shareholder. Prohibited by professional corporation law in many states.

QUORUM

The minimum number or percentage of shareholders or directors authorized by the bylaws to make policy. In lieu of a quorum definition in the bylaws, most states require a simple majority.

REGISTERED AGENT

The person or corporation, legal resident of a state, and sometimes county, in which a corporation conducts a business or practice, and which serves as the legal representative and mailing address for the corporation. Required of alien corporations; optional for domestic corporations.

SEAL, CORPORATE

The uniquely-designed impression embossed on official documents of the corporation.

SECTION 1244 STOCK

A federal statute that allows shareholders to deduct from personal income the full loss in value of shares in their corporation. The status must be declared in advance.

SHAREHOLDER REGISTER AND STOCK TRANSFER BOOK

Official record of stock ownership from first issue through subsequent ownership transfer.

SHARES

The apportionment of a corporation's ownership by equal units based on the total valuation of the corporation divided by the number of shares issued.

SPLIT-DOLLAR PLAN

One involving payments by an employee and by the corporation in a combination that provides greater benefits to employees than would be available if payments were made by the corporation or the employee alone.

STATUTORY ADDRESS

Legal address of a corporation.

STOCK CERTIFICATE

Document indicating a number of shares and ownership of the same.

STOCK OPTIONS

A form of compensation granted to key men by which they can purchase shares at a guaranteed favorable rate for a specified period of time.

STRAIGHT LIFE INSURANCE

See "permanent life insurance."

SUBCHAPTER S

A feature of federal law that allows owners of a small corporation to pass corporate losses on through as deductions against personal income; corporation must also surrender benefits, however. Not likely to be attractive to a professional corporation.

TAXABLE INCOME

Net income minus exemptions and deductions.

TERM INSURANCE

Simple insurance against loss with no return otherwise. Benefits often geared to decreasing need, payoff declining to zero at policy termination.

THIN CORPORATION

One the IRS labels as too thinly capitalized, usually because too much of its capitalization is from loans by owners rather than from purchases of shares.

TICKLER

System of filing action reminders to appear at appropriate moments for effective, efficient handling.

TREASURY STOCK

Shares held by the corporation instead of having been issued or reissued.

VESTED RIGHTS, VESTING

A point in time, by law occurring immediately under a Keogh Plan and within ten years for qualified corporate plans, at which an employee qualifies to receive a pension at retirement.

WAIVER OF MEETING

New policy decisions requiring fast action through a polling of directors by mail or telephone, such new policy validated by waiver of meeting signed by directors. Method of making policy, allowable if authorized by bylaws and permitted by state law.

WHOLE LIFE INSURANCE

See "permanent life insurance."